PowerTribes gives you a thoughtful way to monetize what you know and how you do what you do. So many people end up closing their businesses down without capitalizing on what they built. If you've felt like you have a special way of doing what you do in business – and are looking for a way to capitalize on it – this is the book for you. PowerTribes gives you a step by step paint by numbers action plan, that you can actually implement!

Justin Krane, CFP®, CIMA®
President, Krane Financial Solutions

PowerTribes offers a clear and simple pathway to the goldmine of certification or licensing. His 30+ years of experience shines through as he presents his model in a way that both educates and inspires. I loved his 14 questions that pinpoint the foundation infrastructure required to build a well-run Certification Program. Those questions, on their own, are worth the investment in this book ten thousand times over. Many books are really just brochures padded with a lot of not-so-valuable information. By contrast, PowerTribes offers so many practical steps (not just concepts) including a fully outlined seven-part certification system complete with the identification of 45 sub-systems! PowerTribes is therefore not just a book, but rather a step by step blueprint for multiplying revenue ten-fold and more, by simply tapping into the power of your existing client base.

Tom Poland, Author of Leadsology – The Science of Being In Demand

PowerTribes is a step by step guide on how to build and successfully launch a certification program within your organization to help you turn your best customers into licensed providers of your service to increase your impact and income, approaching the process like an engineer who is planning to build an amazing structure from scratch one step at a time. "

Iman Aghay
Founder and Director, Success Road Academy

PowerTribes a business building tool that will convert your best clients into your raving fans. They will become your unpaid sales force to grow your business. Do yourself, and your business a favor, and learn from Mitch.

Rennie Gabriel, www.WealthOnAnyIncome.com

POWERTRIBES

**How Certification Can Explode Your Business!
The Secret Blueprint that Intuit, Salesforce and
Infusionsoft Use to Generate Big Profits Fast**

by Mitch Russo

LEADERS IN GLOBAL PUBLISHING

Published by Motivational Press, Inc.
1777 Aurora Road
Melbourne, Florida, 32935
www.MotivationalPress.com

Manufactured in the United States of America.

ISBN: 978-1-62865-572-8

CONTENTS

DEDICATION

I WANT TO DEDICATE THIS BOOK TO MY DAD. It was his entrepreneurial drive and skills that he impressed upon me as a young boy that gave me the insatiable desire to create and grow companies. His patience, common sense and genuine approach to dealing with people of all walks of life, helped me to become the man I am now.

INTRODUCTION

Y OU ARE ABOUT TO EMBARK on a journey down a winding river with many swirls and eddies. If you'll stay with the flow, if you'll meet each small twist with a solution, you will be transported to a place few people reach. You will accelerate your sales, revenue, and competitive position, all while decreasing expenses and blowing your profits out of the water. It will never fail, as long as you qualify and do the work.

That's what this book is about. It's a process; a model; a blueprint of my 30 plus years of experience building businesses and Certified Consultant Programs. I am now able to share it with you completely; I hold nothing back. It's all here for you. If you ever find yourself wondering what I meant with any of this content, reach out to me directly at mitch@mitchrusso. com and simply ask.

This book is about using a specific business model called Certification: a systematic way of accomplishing your goals and objectives. Many companies who credit their Certification Program as the key to their long-term market domination, user base expansion, and revenue growth have successfully used it.

Microsoft, Intuit, Salesforce, and Infusionsoft are just a few of the companies who have employed Certification to their benefit and continue to grow their Certification community outside their corporate structure.

If done properly, my system will generate significant benefits that can change how you do business in the most fundamental way. But if mistakes are made or steps are skipped, it can and will cause extreme difficulties for your company.

Today, I build Certification Programs for my clients which share 4 common attributes:

» A successful launch that generates six-figures or more in just 10 days after launching.

» A completely new method of finding new clients and closing more sales.

» The creation of recurring revenue in multiple streams.

» An asset that will potentially double the value of a company and grow to seven figures in less than 2 years.

Some of you who are reading or listening to this book assume you don't have the skills to set up the infrastructure, and others still will not want to take your focus off your current business. But if you're in a position to create a Certification Program, then, 90 days from now, you could be launching your own, following my step-by-step blueprint. You can see more about how I qualify and how to connect with me at www. MyPowerTribe.com.

Let's start with your clients, or customers, first.

Most of us that have clients/customers who initially responded to a promotional offer, something as simple as, "You can use LinkedIn to find new clients," or, "Our product will improve your life/company/business," which is how you first came into contact with your prospects.

By really understanding what, exactly, your client/customer wanted when they first bought your product or service, you will understand what can be taught and certified as a skill or practice.

Your clients are people with various levels of competency. From those who barely used or looked at what you sold them, to those who are pushing you to make your services and products better and better; those people are your most passionate clients, the ones who push the limits. They know your processes, your software, and your material better than 90% of your audience.

This is precisely the group who we will be speaking directly to as we create this new business unit, your Certified Consultant Program, for your company.

Our very first group of people; our pilot program, will come from our existing client base.

You will soon understand what most people don't get: that you have an enormous untapped asset at your very feet. All you have to do is reach down, pick it up, reposition it slightly, and watch as it expands your business dramatically.

It will generate millions of dollars over the years and will become one of the most powerful, profitable business actions you could take. It will give you a nationwide presence in about a year; it will create an unpaid army of sales people that represent your company at the highest level. The best part is that it is very inexpensive to implement compared to the vast opportunity it provides. This is worth your attention, but you have to be careful: small mistakes up front will lead to disaster later.

Trust me on that one. I was on the brink of shutting down and destroying my company's reputation while opening myself to multiple potential lawsuits. I will share that story, along with how I discovered the cause of the problems and how I solved them.

It's time to get into the details and show you everything. I hope you are excited about the possibilities. Let's get started.

CHAPTER ONE

WHAT IS A POWERTRIBE?

I COULD USE THE TERM Certification Program and PowerTribe interchangeably to a point, but there is a big difference. A PowerTribe is a Certification Program built from the perspective of creating the culture first, with or before you create your business model.

We are creating a community, a group of people who have their own goals, their own needs and desires. We want to align our needs with theirs, and we want them to know that we care about them at the highest level. To me, many of my own Certified Consultants from my days at Timeslips Corporation have stayed friends for life. That's what a PowerTribe really is: a group of other human beings who want to help each other, including you. That is what the culture part of this discussion is all about.

The benefits are many. The first is that you sidestep many problems other companies have with their Certification Programs.

Let's look at an example of a Certification Program without a culture:

My friends at a very popular digital marketing company created a training for people who want to be marketing professionals focused on the digital world. They built several very nice training programs, costing between $500 and $1,000. To qualify, you need a credit card, and a pulse. That's it. After you graduate, you receive your certificate, and you're on your own.

Yes, they've sold over 15,000 of these certification products, and yes, the training is good, but how many of those people are successful at building a business? Do they get leads from the program? How many of those people get support from their peers? How many are "in" with others and are learning from the collective wisdom of the group?

As of now, none of that is happening. In fact, someone who was certified in 2014 and has a valid "certificate" may be missing a lot of very recent developments in marketing methodology.

The difference between selling a certificate and building a PowerTribe comes down to two distinct details:

1. BUILDING A BUSINESS MODEL

The goal of any program that I build is to provide members with a new business opportunity. We know what it takes to be successful, which, first and foremost takes great training. We deliver on that, of course. But we also provide something that usually is not provided: lead flow. And in some cases, we provide clients who have been closed and paid. When you offer a program, which has that very important feature, you are offering a systematic way of entering, building, and growing a business. Later, I'll share with you some of the ways we do that.

2. BUILDING A CULTURE

Without a culture, you have a group of independent people who really don't have boundaries. Culture is like the warm embrace of the family that provides boundaries and freedoms, which improves the experience for both the company and the new Certified Consultant or coach. Without having this very powerful set of guidelines, entropy takes over, and that simply destroys what you spent many dollars and hours creating.

I mentioned earlier how my own company almost crashed was all about not having this valuable philosophy in place before I started. Luckily, I was able to salvage several of my best Certified Consultants who were interested in being part of the new world we built right the second time around.

A PowerTribe is unique in that it encompasses all the best practices of a family (without the insanity most of us have experienced) and of a business with great products which are ready to market. A PowerTribe is an asset that sits outside the company and can be monetized directly or indirectly. Like any great sales channel, you can place products into it and they will generate momentum, even if those products are not even yours.

In the chapter called "Deliberately Create Your Culture," we will get deeper into the entire process, and you will clearly see why this is as important as it is.

CHAPTER TWO

HOW TO TELL IF YOU'RE READY FOR A POWERTRIBE

HOW TO TAKE THE NEXT STEP IN BUILDING YOUR CERTIFICATION PROGRAM

As I mentioned in Chapter One, the first group is your early adopters: those who love what you do so much that they'll be the first to buy what you're offering. You will build your program with the early adopters in mind, who want to be Certified in what you do so they can create this "transformation" in other people or companies, just like you did.

You might ask yourself, "Why would I want to create an army of competitors, arm them with my trade secrets and turn them loose on my potential clients?" The simple answer comes in the form of another question: What if you made a percentage of every sale or service performed and multiplied that number by hundreds of people throughout the year?

Soon, I will ask you three questions. If you can answer "Yes" to all three, you are perfectly positioned to take this journey with me.

LET'S FIRST SET THE STAGE FOR SUCCESS.

In most companies, a small percentage of your clients decide they love your products or services so much that they want to do more. Some want to do much more, which they see as a way to transition to a more lucrative career, find a deeper purpose to their work, and/or become part of a group. From time to time, clients may overtly ask you, "How can I learn to do what you do?" This action of bonding with your best clients and leading them to success will be the answer to the waves of profits landing on the shores of your bank account, mostly without your help or participation.

Here's how to position your products for this type of planned ascension, and eventually how to multiply your sales volume using your new Certified Consultant (CC) network and by building multiple streams of revenue.

THE 3 CORE QUALIFYING QUESTIONS:

1. Do you have a process, program, or system that generates a very positive outcome with others? It could be a coaching program, a training course, or a software tool. It can also be a device, such as a medical appliance.

2. Can the system, program, or process be used by others to create the same outcome when they employ it? In other words, if you taught someone else your "thing" or gave them your device with some training, could they get the same results as you?

3. Does your system, process, or tool already have people who've experienced the outcome, and would you estimate that at least 500 people or companies are your customers, clients, or fans?

Question three is only important if you want to immediately fill your pilot program to the maximum limit of 20 people within one week of launching your program. If you don't have 500 clients, you can still build a highly effective and valuable Certification Program, but it will monetize more slowly.

The reason we pick the number 500 is because of the "early adaptor" paradigm, which states that 2 to 5% of your existing customers will want whatever you offer immediately and want be the first to try out your new process, idea, or technology.

With an early adapter mindset, you can see how 500 clients should net about 20 highly motivated, action-oriented candidates for your new Certification Program. That's exactly what we want: a full pilot program.

If you have answered yes to all three questions, then you undoubtedly will be able to build a very viable Certified Consultant (CC) Program. You may call your program by a different name - Certified Coaches, Certified Agents, License Holders; it doesn't matter. All that matters is your answered "yes."

LET'S REVIEW: YOU'RE FIT TO BUILD YOUR OWN PROGRAM, IF...

» You sell software which needs support, customization, and training.

» You've developed a technique on how to buy and sell homes for a profit, and the end user needs your materials as well as training.

» You are a "thought leader" with a book or a process, oriented to help people get to the next level.

» You have a medical, dental, chiropractic, or surgical procedure you have perfected, or an invention that goes along with a technique.

» You have an ongoing training program you build on regularly that teaches others your way of doing something, and which shows results when others apply it.

» You have a process for improving other's business methods; for example, hiring nurses, starting a retail business, or even raising your consciousness – all great candidates for this concept.

» You have a tool (physical, electronic, software, or otherwise) that greatly reduces costs, saves time, enhances results, and requires training.

» You have a tool coupled with a service, such as a credit card authorization terminal that needs to be installed and requires training to best profit from it.

If this is you, then you are a prime candidate to build a Certified Consultant Program, a PowerTribe!

Three years into building Timeslips Corp., we discovered another very powerful software brand that was just starting to take hold. Perhaps you've heard of the software program called "Quicken" that revolutionized the way people managed their checkbooks: it was followed by a more robust version for small businesses called QuickBooks.

Back then, I approached the founder of Intuit, Inc., Scott Cook, to see if we could work together and link my Timeslips software to his accounting products. He was generating about six million dollars per year in revenue at the time, and we were less than half his size. He was very interested in our newly minted, and now very successful, Certified Consultant Program.

Scott asked if I could give him a copy of my entire certification system handbook, and I agreed. When I gave him our system, he built his Certified Consultant Program for accountants who would become certified in QuickBooks, and eventually dwarfed our program with thousands of accountants trained to support the software.

Scott, grateful for my help, returned the favor some years later and enabled us to link our products to QuickBooks, which gave us access to his market filled with CPAs. Eventually, we were able to enter the market, enrolling both accountants and clients as Certified Consultants.

Think about it: if you had a network like this for your company:

» What doors would it open?

» What relationships could you build?

» What alliances could you create?

THIS IS POWER IN THE MOST VISIBLE WAY!

You will have built an army that is loyal to you, and by helping your troops in the field, you are helping your company become more influential in every conversation with your peers.

» What would you do with your Certification Program?

» Who could you influence?

» What alliances would you build if you had this to offer a partner in a marketing relationship?

Year after year, my Certified Consultant Program has opened many large, heavy doors for our little company, helping us achieve our goals much faster than we would have without it. It had given us the equivalent of having a company office in every state without actually spending anything to make that happen. Eventually, other companies wanted access to our network to promote their products.

I didn't gain access to someone else's sales channel, we instead created our own, and you can, too. Our Certified Consultants were loyal to the company because we were helping them build their business.

They benefited greatly being associated with us. We treated them like the "ambassadors" they were; we included them in our activities and made them feel as important as they were. They had *status* inside our world; they were important to our company, and it elevated their position with their clients.

When all was said and done, I had discovered an untapped force of nature, which we never abused or took for granted. As a result, we got to use it!

Did you answer the three questions above with "yes?" Good! Then let's continue.

CHAPTER THREE

THE TIMESLIPS EXAMPLE

Note: This next section is historical, if you are not interested in the background, skip it.

A GRIPPING PROBLEM OPENS a doorway to a surprising new solution. In 1988, my team and I at Timeslips, Corp. discovered a very powerful software brand that was just starting to take hold. In 1988, I approached Scott Cook, founder of Intuit, Inc., to see if we could work together and link my Timeslips software to his revolutionary accounting products. He was generating about $6 million dollars per year in revenue at the time, and we were less than half his size. He was very interested in our newly minted, and now very successful, Certified Consultant Program.

Scott asked if I could give him a copy of my entire certification system handbook, and I agreed. When I gave him our system, he built his Certified Consultant Program for accountants who became certified in QuickBooks, and eventually dwarfed our program with thousands of accountants trained to support the software.

Scott, grateful for my help, returned the favor some years later and enabled us to link our products to QuickBooks, which gave us access to his market filled with CPAs. Eventually, we were able to enter the market, enrolling both accountants and clients as Certified Consultants.

Think about it: if you had a network like this for your company:

» What doors would it open?

» What relationships could you build?

» What alliances could you create?

TIMESLIPS, CORP.: THE ORIGIN STORY

Three years before this, in 1985, I was building Timeslips Corp. to be the largest, most well-known time and billing software vendor in the world. By the time I sold the company at the end of my journey with Timeslips Corp., we had amassed nearly 250,000 users and over 350 Certified Consultants. That was our PowerTribe.

But it almost didn't happen; in fact, creating my first "Consultant" was a result of me almost crashing the company.

In 1985, the personal computer was just starting to come into mainstream use as a true business tool. Spreadsheets and word processors were popular, and everyone loved the productivity gain a PC could deliver.

In that year, I came up with an idea for a software program that would keep track of time, help professionals bill by the hour, and make it so accessible that anyone with a computer could instantly log their work and activities.

While time, billing, and accounting software was already in wide use, our approach was different – so much so that it captured the minds and hearts of many new clients in a very short period. Within 18 months of opening our doors, we were generating over $1 million dollars in sales.

I had to scale our little two-person shop into a viable company with tech support, customer support, and a staff of programmers monitored by several Q/A employees. As costs for manufacturing began to skyrocket with outside vendors, I decided, very quickly, to build my own manufacturing facility to handle the ever-growing demand for our packaged software.

By year three, we had doubled again in sales, but so had our expenses. One of our biggest expenses was running our Tech Support Department, which was growing faster than our sales.

I had a problem: we couldn't spend more without selling more software, and our customers were demanding more of our technical support. Overhead expanded every month as sales decreased with speedy significance. There was no internet, only 1,200-baud modems, and CompuServe was a big idea back then. Customers were starting to demand a higher level of services, such as on-site office visits and live training. Both of those would become one more expense to bear as we struggled to keep up. The stress was mounting.

As a young, inexperienced CEO with no mentor or business advisor, I didn't exactly know what to do. Our problems were only getting worse. I read books searching for some "wisdom" that could provide insight into how to get my company to the "next level," and I discovered a few influential authors back then. One of them was Tom Peters.

I loved how Tom Peters made me feel as I sat in the audience of his blistering rants on how to solve the problems of the day. My favorite memory is of one of his most impressive diatribes during a time when the quality of published software in the general market was so bad that the press was taking notice. Tom would pace back and forth on stage and scream to his audience that it was our fault the quality was so bad; it was the CEO's fault for not making quality the #1 priority in the company.

Tom had a unique solution: his advice was to buy six books on software quality, place them on my desk with the spines facing out, and then call my developers into my office and pepper them with questions about why the quality of our products was not where it should be. Rinse and repeat, week after week. The point was to show my team that quality was important to me. I was to stay focused on this approach for several months or longer as the complexity of our code base grew.

Of course, we had beta testers, and they were helpful, but none worked at it enough to make a dent. We also began to hire Quality Assurance people to dig deeper into solving the problems each new release seemed to bring.

Tom Peters taught me something simple: the solution to my problems is sometimes already there, and by shifting my perspective just a little, I would be able to see them. That was the jewel that Tom gave me, and it has stayed with me all my life.

At the time, however, we still needed help. We needed more support people, and we needed more sales. We hit a plateau where we just couldn't increase sales more than a few percent, no matter what we did, without taking our ad budget to the next level.

I was also running around the country from stage to stage, appearing live at PC User Groups (which were popular back then), all of which was taxing my already tight schedule.

There were several sleepless nights where I tossed and turned, burdened by this slowly consuming problem of how to ease the support burden on my company. My partner, Neil, was keenly aware of the problem as well, and was constantly working on the user interface to smooth it out, add more contextual help dialogues, and eliminate any areas of confusion.

TIME CHECK: 1989.

Still no internet, and retail software was sold just like books, with the same distribution channels. The only exception was the specialty software distributor, Kenfil. They serviced our largest account, Egghead Discount Software, which was, at the time, moving about 500 copies a month and growing slowly.

This was the turning point for my company and me.

We received a call from a client who demanded we visit her office to "fix" her computer, which she claimed was crashed by our software. This was an important client, one who had a lot of influence with the California Bar Association. At that time, lawyers amounted to 75% of our market.

Flying a support staff member to San Francisco seemed like the only viable solution. That was an expensive fix, which cost more than the client had paid for their software. But it had to be done and done well, or our reputation would have been scarred. We sent someone out, and that solved her problem, yet cost us several thousand dollars in wages and expenses.

I explained this for one important reason. I was living on the edge of this business; it was the most important thing in my life, and I would protect it with all my energy from real or imagined problems. Being a young CEO meant that I didn't have any experience, and that I had to make it up as I went along. This was my solution. Crisis averted, but at what cost?

Several weeks later, I received a call from another law firm client who had lost their database in a hard disk crash but blamed it on the software. They demanded that I show up on site and fix it immediately. Here again, more expenses, and not much to show for it.

My personal policy was that I would never leave a customer unhappy, and I was known to go to any end to solve the problem. Even if the cost of my software was only $99 at the time, my reputation was worth far more.

Then it hit me: Why not find out who my most skilled, most knowledgeable clients are in the same geographic local as this law firm and ask – no, beg – them to drive over and take a look, as a favor to me. I did just that: I spoke to a very smart, friendly office manager named Ann from a firm across town, and she was thrilled that I, the President of Timeslips Corp., would think of her to ask this favor.

With a deep breath and a sigh of relief, I dispatched her and asked her to call me back, at home if need be, with a progress report. I checked my watch every 15 minutes, knowing she was on-site and imagining how this could have been a terrible mistake. I didn't call to "check in" because that would look a little desperate on my part. That night, several hours after most people had gone home, I heard from Ann with the news.

She had recovered the database using a disk recovery program, rebuilt it for the client, and the client was thrilled. It turns out that it was not Timeslips that crashed her system, it was just the nature of hard drives, and of course the client didn't have a backup. When the client asked how much it would cost that day, Ann said it was a favor that "Mitch Russo asked me to do." As soon as she said it, the client reached into his pocket and handed her a $100 bill. She accepted gracefully and floated all the way home.

When she called and told me the story of how angry and upset my client was, and specifically what she had accomplished over the course of the next few hours, I couldn't have been more relieved. Then she said something I didn't expect: "Please let me know if you have anyone else I can help, I'd love to!"

I felt a wave of peace settling over me as I finally had a good night's sleep, knowing that my client was happy again and that Ann had stepped up to help.

I slept well but woke up with a startling idea. What would happen if I had more than one "Ann" out there to help with more clients? Why not create an army of Anns who can service my clients locally?

This was the genesis of our Timeslips Certified Consultant Program. I went back to the library to research how to test and certify people, and I found several examples-- none of which were very good. Finally, I decided to create a comprehensive test that I could place in the hands of my best clients. If they passed, I could "certify" them as capable of supporting our users.

I had to figure this all out on my own, and admittedly I made many, many mistakes along the way.

I did send out that test to a few people we identified as competent users of our software; I received most of them back, and most people failed the test. Others had heard about the test and started to request it as a way of training their staff. This gave me an idea.

"LIGHT DAWNS ON MARBLEHEAD."

Maybe that's a Boston joke; Marblehead, MA is a beautiful coastal community that is known for amazing sunrises. Later, that expression evolved to have the same meaning as, "I coulda had a V8!"

I realized at that moment that we should be selling tests, not giving them away. But to turn it into a product, we needed to create a study guide, which came promptly after I announced the idea to my staff. Calling this a "certification" would be considered a stretch today.

We started to monetize this process.

We announced this by sending a letter to our installed base. Back then we had customers who had to register their software by sending in a postcard, which we plugged into our database. At that time, we probably had about 15,000 customers. Six days later, the mail truck arrived with a full bin of order forms, all containing a check for $750, of which $500 was refundable if they failed the test. More than we expected; selling tests was starting to become a nice little business that hadn't been there before.

Fast-forward about six months. By that time, over a hundred clients had been served by our new Certified Consultants (CCs,) and the news was mixed, at best. Some CCs were competent, but many were not. Furthermore, some had not paid attention to their personal hygiene, while others were just, in a word, "bad." The sale of tests was growing, and our base number of "Certified" Consultants stood at about seventy-five.

I was not happy with the results. I didn't want one single client to ever have a bad experience with a Timeslips Certified Consultant, and it was happening more frequently. Clearly, there was something wrong with the testing process; the training process; the screening process; or all the above.

I had to stop the sale of tests since my clients were in jeopardy. I needed to discover and fix what we had done wrong. Why did those people pass tests and still "fail" at the client site? I had to ask myself three questions:

1. How could I "fix" all the problems that my new Certified Consultants had made?
2. How could they not have had the sensibility to brush their teeth or shower, or show up on time?
3. Why would they show up in shorts and a T-shirt at a professional office?

I requested a log of all the complaints we had received, and I personally started to call clients and ask what they experienced. Some of it was funny and scary at the same time; while several people told me how wonderful their experience was on the consulting side; some CCs just didn't present well. We called over 60 clients over the course of six weeks and compiled a detailed list of all the things that could go wrong.

It all came down to two things: we lacked a community structure for our Certified Consultants, and we also lacked very specific training on the nuances of how to act like a professional service provider. We also discovered that our CCs were not very good at marketing their services. We realized what we had to do: provide very specific instructions on every element of how they conduct themselves and run their business.

Our training binder had copies of all the communication we could think of for our Certified Consultants to do business as a professional service company. We had to write the engagement letters for our CCs and tell them when to call to confirm appointments and literally what to say. We covered things such as how to dress, how to arrive on time, and what NOT to say to clients.

But, now we had a new problem: how do we deal with the technical problems of education?

Some CCs were so bad that we had to eject them from the program. One exhibited signs of psychotic behavior that required us to call the police. Many of our newly-grown base of CCs were helping to test our software as "beta testers," and that was something we highly valued. We had some very smart people out there, and their help was invaluable. Several of our CCs were working office managers who moonlighted as consultants; several left their companies to become full-time consultants and started training on companion software like QuickBooks.

After an exhaustive review and revamping of our training program, I decided there was only one thing left to do. I would invite our growing group of CCs to spend four days with us at the King's Grant Hotel in Beverly, MA, for technical training, sales training, community building, and lots of fun.

As expected, most of those who came that first year were thrilled to meet us, delighted to feel part of the company, and looking forward to a new experience. We poured our heart and soul into training them at the highest level, understanding the problems they were having, and offering as much help as we could to make them better at their chosen profession.

The Certified Consultant Symposium was a huge success. The reviews we received were off the charts; people loved the experience, and we loved having them with us for those four days. The after-effects started to show up the week after they departed.

Tech support call volume was stabilizing, and clients universally loved working with our Certified Consultants. Also, sales volume of our support contracts from this new channel was beginning to move the needle.

Yes, even our CCs sold our support contracts; they earned a small commission, but it was mostly so they wouldn't be on the hook for a multitude of daily calls. They reinforced how important it was to have a support contract and, once again, we watched as support contract sales grew.

CCs were starting to have an impact in other areas of the company, as well. I mentioned earlier that I appeared at PC User Groups all over the country, which I enjoyed doing AND which boosted the company's visibility. Interestingly, CCs started to show up, too. I soon decided to invite them to dinner at a restaurant near the venue and get to know those in each location I visited. This turned out to be one of the most satisfying things I've ever done to foster loyalty and friendship.

My dinners were getting popular. Once, we had nearly 20 people show up for one of my Los Angeles dinners, which became almost four hours of camaraderie and suggestions for improving the program and the software, as well as story-telling about how funny some of their client visits were. We laughed, we cried, and we hugged at the end of these sessions.

Our CCs were becoming more important and more loyal than most of our employees.

Finally, we had figured it all out and perfected our Certification Program. The following year, we raised our prices and expanded our offerings, and newly minted Certified Consultants were graduating at the pace of about twenty a month. We were now clearly focused on its success, so I hired a CC program manager into a full-time position in our company.

CC applications with checks began to flood into the company once more. Problems were solved quickly, and we knew how to "fire" a CC who just wouldn't get in line with the program.

Around this same time, our CCs were asking us if they could resell our software. Worried at first about channel conflict, we refused, until one CC came to me with an order for 125 copies. Like I said before, I wasn't very experienced, and I had made many mistakes. Luckily, this was one I could easily correct. I agreed and gave my CCs a 30% discount; my distribution discount was 40%, so I thought I could sneak this through without a conflict.

My CCs were anxious to make money selling my products as well as reaching new clients who could hire them for consulting services. There were also several CCs interested in running ads for their services and offering a product for sale, as well. In response, we produced a complete kit of "artwork" they could duplicate for use in their own ads.

Because we demanded recertification every year, the next year we had double the number of people at our Symposium and our CC ranks had almost tripled. We were generating revenue from this wonderful group of people who loved helping our clients while selling our software and our support contracts.

By our third Symposium, we had over 350 Certified Consultants, where over 200 a year showed up for the annual Symposium. Just to stress how big a deal these Symposiums were to the company, we went overboard to ensure our CCs had a blast. We had a banquet and served incredible food, and even supplied entertainment.

We worked hard, spending many hours on software instruction and new feature demonstration. Our CCs loved that they would get a peek at new features that were not yet available in the software, many of which were a result of their requests. Sometimes, as we showed new features during our training sessions, we would say, "Alan, are you in the room? This is from your recommendation!" and Alan would glow with pride as everyone clapped.

The closing remarks by me were very meaningful to everyone, including myself. I started with a Q&A where anyone could ask me anything, and I was always completely transparent about the answers, even on sensitive subjects. Finally, I spoke about what I expected in the following year regarding trends that would affect them and how they should prepare.

After each Symposium, we noticed a 90-day wave of sales increases, which stabilized at a higher norm than before. Every month our recertification fees would pour in. The compliments and endorsements from our clients were now approaching the hysterical level of true love for our company. We had a long hallway where every testimonial was stapled to the wall. Eventually, we had over a thousand, and we ran out of wall space.

Every time I spoke publicly, my CCs would come out in force to support me. They brought their own clients to my events to hear me speak. I openly acknowledged my CCs as my secret weapon in the war against our competitors. After all, with hundreds of CCs spread all over the country, we had unwittingly created an "army" of salespeople who paid us for the privilege of selling and supporting our software.

Life was hectic, but the results were there. Our little company had grown up to the point where we became one of the leading vendors of technology to the legal community. Even the accounting community was starting to use our software, and we had over fifty different service professions listed as part of our user group.

We had accomplished a lot in just nine years, and we were still having fun. But my partner Neil wanted to move past Timeslips Corporation, and I saw the writing on the wall; it was time to sell the company, and we did. That happened in 1994, the same year my daughter was born.

Our CCs were sad to see that happen; they were afraid they would lose what they spent years building. Sadly, some of them did lose that connection to the company when new owners focused more on profits than thrilling their clients.

The acquiring owner did not place the same level of importance on the client relationship and our CC program as we did. As a result, our CCs received less attention, and many drifted away.

Then, in 1996, after my two-year earn-out was over, I was invited to stay with Sage as the Chief Operating Officer of Sage US. I was up for the challenge, and I stayed another two years as the COO; but I decided it was not the right environment for me, and I left.

As I write these words, just yesterday, December 6th, 2015, I received a note on LinkedIn from a Timeslips beta tester who helped with the original software release back in 1985. I personally knew about 10,000 of my clients, which grew to almost 250,000 by the time I left Sage in 1998. Because of social media, I am still in touch with several dozen of my original CCs. They are constantly reminiscing about the good times they had in Beverly, MA at our Symposiums and their appreciation for what we created.

Why is all this background important?

Because without that accidental discovery of a way to create a third-party network of this independent channel of unpaid professionals, who rewarded us every year with fees, tech support assistance, and undying admiration, I would have just had a software company that sold a product. I would never have established a massive national presence or build an "invisible" sales channel, becoming the company's third largest source of revenue. I would never have found a way to effectively help so many of my clients, who greatly benefited from our CCs who help them run their busy offices more efficiently. And I never would have sold my company for more than eight figures or reached the level of national penetration and dominance that I did. Because of building our CC program, the value of my company almost doubled in just two and a half years.

That was my "PowerTribe." Those were our people. We loved them, and they loved us.

Let's summarize:

We had a software company with basically one product and a support contract, which was not very popular.

We had escalating expenses, a growing user base, and a lot of demand for support, which we were struggling to fulfill.

We accidentally discovered that by dispatching a very competent local user of our products to the office of another client who was having problems with our software, we could help more clients. The Certified Consultant Program was born.

We scaled this into a series of paid actions that attracted the top 3- 5% of our user base, who would:

» Spend money on Certification annually.
» Pay us to train them yearly at a live Symposium.
» Become our third largest sales channel.

- » Extend our brand deeper into our market and other adjacent markets at no cost to us.

- » Act as unpaid quality assurance teams.

- » Reduce the burden on our company for tech support.

- » Aggressively sell our own support contracts.

- » And enjoy having this relationship with the company and the executives, which has lasted a lifetime for many.

Because of that discovery and the resulting success it created for our company, we were able to scale our business much faster than ever before. We were able to create a nationwide "footprint" and presence in every major city and build sales and support for our product without spending anything to make it happen.

Our competitors were shocked that we had developed this nationwide presence in just three years. It became our competitive edge; the personality and culture of the company were mirrored by the best of our CCs.

This was my first "PowerTribe," and I hope this is the start of your own private revolution to accomplish all that and more.

CHAPTER FOUR

MAPPING OUT YOUR PLAN

START WITH UNDERSTANDING YOUR STRENGTHS AND WEAKNESSES

As THE CEO OF Business Breakthroughs International and a partner with Chet Holmes and Tony Robbins, I regularly maintained a series of mind maps so I could always "see" where we would potentially lose a prospect or client opportunity. The first time through the process of mapping out our selling strategy, I was shocked to see how many "leaks" and stubs were present.

I highly recommend regularly building and updating your own mind map to "see" (if you are a visual person) where all the customer and prospect paths lead, how to augment them and find sales shortcuts to increasing revenue. When I work with private clients, this is the very first thing we do together, create this two-dimensional model of their entire business. With that tool, we can easily see lost opportunities, areas of concern and new channels of possibilities for inserting a Certified Consultant program.

Inspect your mind map to locate where you think a PowerTribe member could be connected into the loop. They can add value by enhancing the sale, saving a prospect, selling something different that's synergistic, or simply helping your new client do a better job of fully utilizing your product/service.

If you've never done this before, you might be surprised how powerful of an exercise this can be. By creating your plan, you get to inspect every assumption made about how you sell, how you prospect, how you monetize your client base, and what mistakes you may have made. Even if you don't build a PowerTribe, this exercise is an excellent way to dive deeply into your sales and marketing process, even if you are a relatively new company.

Follow these steps to begin:

Answer these questions as thoroughly and carefully as possible. This is the foundation required when building the infrastructure to support a well-run Certification Program.

1. How many ways do you attract prospects to the company? Please list them.

2. What happens as each prospect enters your world?

3. What do they receive, when, and for how long? List all steps that take place.

4. What happens when a new client makes a purchase? How do you communicate with them, what do they receive, and who in your company speaks to them?

5. What happens to prospects who have been solicited over and over again, but don't buy? When do you stop communicating? Do you delete them from your list?

6. What is the next thing you sell to someone once they buy your product or service?

7. How much time passes before they are making another purchase?

8. How long does this cycle continue with your customer stepping up and buying again?

9. Do you have a sales force or a sales farce? Are they effective at closing sales, and do you compensate them mostly on performance or mostly through base pay?

10. Are they outbound calling, live visits, or something else?

11. How much (as a percentage of top line revenue) does each product contribute to your bottom line?

12. Who is your first line of defense when a customer has a problem?

13. Besides offering a solution when customers or clients have a problem, is there an up-sell offer?

14. Do you classify prospects in your CRM systems, describing how and when (and how many times) you contact every person with detailed call logs or communication logs?

All of this data will be used to create a mind map and a flow chart that you can use to see how sales and prospects flow through your system. This should reveal some new information, which is very relevant to building your PowerTribe and can greatly affect your closing rate with prospects.

As you start to lay this out in a mind map or flow chart, you will encounter dead ends or "stubs" where items (customers, prospects, leads, requests for services) appear to be at a dead end. It's good to locate stubs in each branch, since you can recapture those lost opportunities and use them to salvage a relationship; you can even use them to make a sale, or better train your staff.

Chet Holmes in his book The Ultimate Sales Machine pioneered the term Sales Superstar as a specific personality type. I later took Chet's process and refined it, put a system in place to streamline it and used it for all our hiring at Business Breakthroughs, International. I wrote a detailed overview of how to hire Sales Superstars on my blog. Here's the article I wrote: https://mitchrusso.com/how-to-hire-sales-superstars/

Give them dead (unconverted) leads and have them attempt to revive them. Make sure you record those calls; the learning experience alone will be very valuable. Also, don't forget that because even though someone didn't buy from you now, they may still buy from you in the future.

Now that you've identified the stubs, find a way to either recirculate or reconnect that stub back into the prospect or sales flow, so you don't lose them completely.

For example, a stub or a dead end in your flow chart would be when a prospect is new to your company and does not buy after several attempts. Many people would stop trying to sell to them after a number of offers. My suggestion would be to move them to a different path so they are always hearing about new products, new services, and new offers. They may buy the same thing you originally offered in the future if you stay in touch and continue to develop that relationship.

Today, you can greatly enhance the way you interact with prospects while accelerating growth and adding several new revenue channels. With the internet, trust can build quickly, and new relationships can be formed with strong bonds without ever meeting face-to-face.

Today, when I work with my clients, we start out by defining the business model.

More than anything else, the business model drives the entire process. Without having completely mapped out your business model and all its components first, you won't accomplish your goals. You will find yourself stuck with a network of members who may get angry, upset, and/or disappointed because your program is not what you said it would be or giving them the benefits they were expecting.

What we look for first and foremost is how we can insert the presence of a Certified Coach or Consultant into the sales and prospecting system to benefit everyone involved, including the company itself.

This is where we start because with this foundation, everything we do will be guided by the process of fulfilling the goals and plans we set out to accomplish when we began.

This plan starts with understanding how prospects and customers flow into and through your company. A great company generates lots of prospects and then converts a high percentage of them into clients. On the surface, that's what we see. But going deeper, we find there are systems in place to accomplish this.

You probably already have those CRM systems with lead generation and auto-responders to escalate the level of promotion as prospects become more responsive to your offers. A percentage of those prospects NEVER become clients. We call those DEAD LEADS. But are they really dead? Some are, but many didn't convert because the timing wasn't right.

What about your existing clients; can they benefit by working directly with a Certified Consultant? I am sure that some can, and many will be interested to know they could when the time is right.

When your existing clients work with your Certified Consultants, you can share in the fees they bill. What about past clients, could they be reactivated if you had a Certified Consultant they could work with? What would happen if you offered past clients a chance to buy your product and get time with your CC for free?

Let's keep going. What other groups that you are associated with would want to know about your new Certified Consultant program?

Do you have trade shows or events? Why not put together a small 30-minute educational opportunity for anyone who wants to become a

Certified Consultant, making it so they can walk away with an application right from your booth?

How about your social media? You can use social media in a variety of ways, from announcing your new program to showcasing a few of your CCs over the course of several months.

I mentioned before that you can share in the revenue from your Certified Consultant's assignments. Ideally, you can set up sales pages to which CCs can send a client and have them enroll themselves into a coaching program or hire the CC for a particular project. The money goes through your system, and they get paid a portion.

In terms of Public Relations, you can create a series of press releases to announce your program which also shines a bright light on your own services and products at the same time. Also, issue a press release with every new Certified Consultant who graduates your program. That press release will be picked up by local press in their community and serve as an announcement of their new service offerings.

Let's go one step further. How about finding an intern or admin person who would use your list of Certified Consultants and locate local speaking opportunities for each? Imagine the delight when he or she finds out that they are booked to speak at their local business round table, bar association meeting, or even as a guest at Vistage meetings. There are many other opportunities for speaking that your intern can locate.

Do you think your Certified Consultants will appreciate that? I bet they would.

As you can see, we have plenty of opportunities to drive clients to our Certified Consultants as we build out our business model.

Inspect your chart to locate where you think a Certified Consultant could be connected into the loop. Once they are plugged in, they can add value by enhancing the sale, saving a prospect, selling something different that's synergistic, or simply helping your new client do a better job of fully utilizing your product/service.

The CEO of LinkedSelling, Josh Turner, who has built a thriving new company, contacted me because I offered to help him with his webinar conversion. I had presided over a team of webinar presenters who were closing at a 40% rate, and he wanted to know how we did that.

After I had spent some time rewriting his sales page, we started to talk about how he can unleash the trapped revenue opportunities he had but didn't recognize. Josh, being a brilliant strategist, immediately saw the value that a Certified Consultant program would bring to his company, and he hired me to make that happen for him.

I started with the same process I just outlined for you above. I did this to discover where to best position their Certified Consultants, so they can generate maximum impact to the company. I also reviewed with him how I did this at Timeslips Corp., and what the results were.

Josh was smart enough to see the opportunity, and he provided the resources I needed to get the work done inside his company. With his trust, we created a powerful "launch" of his CC program.

Josh says in his testimonial:

"We started working with Mitch just a few months ago, and from the get-go we worked with him designing the entire plan and the roll-out. Mitch has worked very closely with myself and my team to build the program, including all the training curriculum as well as the marketing, and putting a plan together for how we are actually going to get people into the program, which is obviously a critical component of the whole thing."

"Along the way, Mitch has been excellent to work with. He's been extremely responsive, and his expertise has really been invaluable in helping us get this program off the ground. As of just recently, we finally launched the program; I say finally, but it only took us a couple of months to put the whole thing together. Considering it can definitely be a seven-figure-a-year program for us and will expand our business in a ton of different ways, that's not much [time] at all."

THE CORE COMPONENTS OF YOUR PROGRAM:

Before creating your program, you will need some specific documents to use with your applicants during the screening and application process.

There are both legal and ethical issues you must address up-front for you to create your program on solid ground. This means that if you don't go forward using these documents, you will not be protected along many different fronts.

You need to make it clear that your newly-enrolled CCs will not be independent contractors or employees, as I explained earlier. You also must make it clear that they have a responsibility to uphold and protect the copyrights, brand, and reputation of the company.

There is one other aspect to setting up your application process: you must find a way to communicate the company's values and mission as clearly as possible. The goal of bringing on any new Certified Consultant is to ensure they fit into the culture of the company and are the right personality type for inclusion.

There are several important tools to accomplish this, which we will introduce in the screening process. But it is important to use all of these tools as you are building your screening process, so only those who you want as CCs will be included. To be effective, to be ethical, and to be legal, we are going to need some tools.

These are our most powerful tools available:

1. **The Code of Ethics.** If you use a code of ethics (I supply one customized for my clients), introduce it in the screening process. This establishes what you believe are the core values of your company, and you explain exactly how you expect your CCs to act in all foreseeable circumstances. I cannot stress enough how important this is, and how it can be used to clean up difficult situations with both staff and consultants. Furthermore, when you explain what you expect in advance, there are no excuses for "questionable" behavior later. This document is also used to establish the culture of your group in an open, honest, up-front way.

2. **The Certified Consultant Legal Agreement.** If you don't have one, you are asking for problems that can, at worst, shut down your company and, at best, leave you in a dangerous position with the various state agencies. I supply for my clients a specialized, customized legal template, written by my law firm, expressly for this purpose. I highly suggest that you contact your lawyer and get one drawn up immediately or work with me and I will provide you a legal template you can customize for your own needs.

3. **The Personality Test.** I have created a special personality test for my clients to use when screening candidates. You can locate several that range in price from free to several hundred dollars which will allow you to spot distinctly different personality types as you move through the screening process. This will prepare you for what's coming your way. I have used them for years hiring hundreds of people personally, and I wouldn't operate without one, especially knowing what they are capable of.

4. **The Background Check.** For the safety of the company and the others who enroll in the program, your job is to make it safe for anyone and everyone. That starts with knowing precisely who you

have in your program. You can't accept someone just because they are smart enough to answer some questions on a test.

It's on YOU to make sure everyone is an ethical player, so you don't poison the well, so to speak. Background checks are inexpensive; a thorough one will cost around $200. There's one more check you need to run before you decide to move forward: a social media check. This check must be done internally rather than hired out; I don't know of any company that is competent in doing this kind of check.

A social media check means that you have to review all of their Facebook pages (people can have many these days;) you must also review their LinkedIn page, check to see if they have a Tumblr, Twitter, Instagram, and/or Snapchat account, and perform a deep and thorough Google search. There may be more I have not mentioned. Find them all, read them, and look for signs of someone who is not a fit for your organization. Be thorough, because your clients will be, as well. And if they find something undesirable, those people will be "associated" with your company, and that's not a good thing.

If they pass through your screening, then make sure they understand the documents they are about to sign. I suggest a short video followed up by a conversation to ensure they fully understand what they are about to sign.

THE CC LEGAL CONTRACT:
Your Primary Legal Agreement With Your Certified Consultants

As a quick overview, the contract should cover a non-disclosure agreement protecting your IP. It should also detail the nature of the relationship, so they know they are not independent contractors or employees. Your contract should also explain how they will receive payments from clients if that is part of your program design. None of this should be neglected, skipped, or glossed over by you, because of its importance to keeping within the law.

You will need to make it clear to your applicants that what you are doing is not a franchise operation. Once again, your local law firm can ensure that your agreement is clear about this. If you are found infringing on Franchise Law, you won't be happy, so take care of this up front.

In some extreme cases and in some states, this program may be interpreted as crossing the line of "franchise law." It is my understanding that the system I describe in this book should not cross this line, but it's important to pay attention to the details, which is why I urge you not to rely on anyone's templates, including my own, as the last word for your company.

One of the best ways I know of to ensure that you don't infringe on franchise law is to use a franchise questionnaire form to fully disclose your Certified Consultant program, making sure every detail is explained. With this signed by every new CC, odds are that any inquiries will be quickly shut down.

You also must make it clear that your CCs are not Independent Contractors or employees. I can't stress this enough because of its importance in keeping the company safe. I highly recommend making sure that all CCs have a Federal Tax ID number, which means they are a Subchapter S or LLC business. Once again, we are not interested in hiring just anybody, and we don't want Independent Contractors. We need an arms-length relationship with our CCs, so classifying them as a "vendor" is currently the safest way I know of to build that legal wall between you and them. You must make sure your law firm scrutinizes your CC agreement to ensure you are not operating outside the boundaries of the law.

If you understand how important and valuable these tools are, you are ready to begin creating your strategy map. Without it, we can't project with any confidence what will work and what may fail.

Please note: I am not an attorney or an accountant. Be sure to confirm that everything you read here is accurate and applies to your own circumstances in your own state. For my direct clients, I provide full legal agreements written by my own legal counsel as well as the entire code of ethics.

BUILDING THE MAP

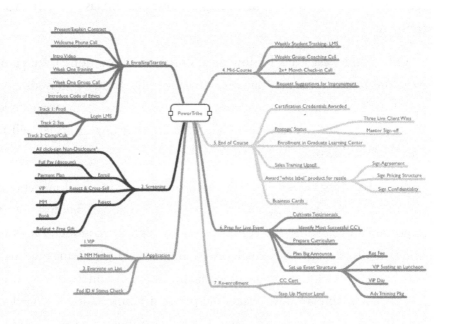

For more examples of different maps, go to: <u>PowerTribesBook.com/maps</u>.

This is a map of the process you will build so that you can "see" every aspect of how your program will work, as discussed above.

I believe that it is important to map out the prospect and client flow through the company because we need to find entry points where injecting the presence of a CC would be most effective. This way, expenses can be cut and profits enhanced, and market domination can grow as a result.

Without that map, there's no clear vision of how to integrate a fully functional network as well as get the most from it.

There are seven elements of planning a program. Each phase must be fully explored and detailed before ANY work can be done. If this is done incorrectly, incompletely, or out of sequence, you won't get the results you want, and you will have to fix it later. Rushing through this step would be foolish and shortsighted.

Because I didn't go through this carefully planned sequence the first time I tried to launch, I almost irreparably damaged my company, and it took a solid year to recover. Learn from my mistakes.

THE PROGRAM FLOW MAP STEPS

Each "Topic" or "Branch" of your mind map is supposed to completely encapsulate everything about that function in one place. This is not hard to do, but it must be comprehensive. Do not skip this step with a short checklist, or worse, think you can keep it all in your head. You can't, so don't try. Otherwise, you will miss critical elements that are vital to a successful program.

1. THE APPLICATION PROCESS BRANCH

Who are you attracting to the program? Have you already identified your VIPs, your clients, your prospects, and maybe other "adjacent" tribes from other companies? Come up with a list for each, as we will want to create a "flow" diagram of how we will reach each of them. What they will receive (sequence), and what you are instructing them to do once they express interest, is fully mapped out.

Work this out in advance but be careful not to overcommit to time-consuming personal interviews for all of those categories; maybe make these exclusive for your VIPs only. Many companies have a mastermind program. These, too, are excellent candidates if they are not busy running their own companies. Just be sure to list each "audience" you have with the company and make sure you note the size, value (regarding revenue), and perceived opportunity.

Once you have that, create a flow diagram for each group. Several groups may have similar flows through the company, but make a note of them all and, in particular, how they are different.

If you have clients and prospects, document where they came from. Did you get them through JV launches? Advertising? Referrals? Facebook group members? The source will remind you of all the various ways you attract people to your company.

As you build your mind map and lists, be sure to note where in your process you screen them. Ideally, you don't want to invest too much time or money before you know they are a good fit.

Now that you have a clear idea as to where your clients and prospects come from, you can see who your most likely source of CC applicants will be.

When you finally get to interview them, both inquire about and educate your applicants on what you are looking for.

A reminder:

Never assume that because a person who "sounds" professional truly is. That's why I do extensive background checks before I hire, which is worth mentioning again in this section of the book. You cannot believe what one discovers when this happens. Also, always have students demonstrate for competence to prove they have absorbed and can apply the material.

Once, I hired an individual who had a Facebook page with very strong right-wing opinions on gun control and other very explosive topics. Worse, this person happily invited clients to "like" his Facebook page and friend him!

That was a major failure on our part; we should never have let him into the program, but we didn't do that all-important social media check to ensure he was acting within our own professional values.

Notice that with all I've mentioned, I've never said anything about a resume. If they are one of your clients who know and love your products and are interested in becoming a Certified Consultant for all the right reasons, then we "should" have an excellent candidate.

The reason we don't need resumes is that we don't care about what they did before, so long as they have the right personality and skills to join our team. This is a crucial mistake many companies make. So let's make sure we are using a very powerful personal assessment to determine if they are a fit, as well.

The most powerful assessments I've found are available on the PowerTribesBook.com website and can be used inexpensively for candidates before you accept them into the program. It's your responsibility to know the nature of every individual before they get involved with your company.

2. THE SCREENING PROCESS BRANCH

After you've fully worked out your application process, the next question to ask your team is: how do we conduct our first screening to ensure we get only our ideal candidates into our program? This step requires that we know who the ideal candidates are.

Knowing they can pay is not the first test, but obviously, they cannot join if they cannot pay. What else is important? Do they need to know a foreign language? Do they need to be a doctor or have a license of some sort? Do they need a certain number of years' experience? All these are part of the initial screening process.

To get through the screen, an applicant must qualify based on your standards for how they need to qualify.

Once you decide they are probably a fit, there is still more work to do. In this final screen, I highly recommend you do a background check on everyone who has been tentatively approved.

As mentioned above, I recommend using a third-party company that specializes in this process. I typically order a criminal background check, a credit check, a sex offender check, and a full social media audit. The social media audit should also be double checked by your staff because it's so important.

Then, finally, you can have them take a personality test. As I mentioned earlier, the personality test is quite revealing and can help you anticipate their needs and issues before we get involved with them.

One more very interesting test: I think it's worthwhile to find out their "why." Knowing their reason for wanting this position will help us know in advance how to best frame problems and solutions so they can fully act in everyone's best interest.

Next, figure out what happens when you reject an applicant. These may be people who love you, love your company, and have been loyal customers for years. It is very important that this process is very carefully thought out and very clearly scripted for your staff as they go through the process of handling and screening candidates.

When you reject a candidate for something other than not having money, it is a good practice to give them a small gift for applying. This is typically a copy of your book, personally signed and sent to their home, a course you sell for real money, or an offer to help them in another way, such as coaching them during that call on how to qualify should they decide to apply again.

Now, what happens when they pass through your entire screening process? What exactly do you have set up for them next? You can't wait around for buyer's remorse to kick in; you need to deliver something instantly, something that gets your newly enrolled student excited. It's okay if you delay the start date for a great reason, such as, "We are going to start everyone at the same time for this class so that you will have peers in the program. You will all start next Monday but read this (or watch this) between now and next week." This could be an overview of how the company works, how your products interact with clients, or testimonials from those who have passed through your program and are very happy with the results.

The next part is to create your "Starting the Program" welcome video that gets sent as soon as they are accepted and pass through the screening process. This is an informative video detailing exactly what they can expect as the training begins. Also, schedule a welcome teleconference. Plan now what you will cover when you have your whole pilot class assembled and ready to start.

As part of the process of enrolling new members into your training environment, make sure you create a video explaining in detail what your culture is all about. It shouldn't be short; it should be comprehensive in scope, covering all of the points you want to make. The culture which you are now deliberately creating will become part of your startup phase for all new applicants and will be a core foundational piece for years to come. It's something that can be revised from time to time as you discover elements of your culture you want to fix or improve.

Finally, depending on when and how you've delivered the contract, I would suggest a video overview of the contract explaining exactly what you want to accomplish with them signing it.

3. ENROLLING/STARTING BRANCH

Here is where you detail exactly what happens when they start the program. There are many details to address, and it's important we don't lose anyone between finishing the screening process and the start of the program. Your program is housed and administered through your Learning Management System, LMS for short.

Later, we will cover in detail how to build your Learning Management System. But for this planning step, we assume it's done and ready to be used.

Building a "custom application" is a great idea. It can be something that only your CCs use to get client engagements done more quickly. It's where they go to set up their new client engagement and should be essential to service the client at the highest level.

The goal of this custom application is to make your company "sticky," so if CCs want to do this type of work, they will need your company to facilitate the technology back-end; in turn, this makes their work go more smoothly. I also advocate a Customer Relationship Management (CRM) software system set up just for CCs so they can take detailed notes on every client interaction. Your CRM system also keeps an accurate account of all emails sent to clients, which you can inspect anytime you want.

In this branch, we want to cover all the information a new student will need to feel comfortable going through the program, and that will provide us with the safety of knowing they understand our contract and how it applies to them. There's a separate section on how to present the contract, but for now, make sure it's part of your enrollment process.

It is here that we welcome them into our program with a video from you, the CEO, and a welcome call from the Program Manager. This is the person who will, day to day, manage the program and be our new student's first point of contact.

As they get going, pair them up with an accountability partner, someone else in the program they can work with as they progress through the training. I have built a system to specifically match and guide accountability partners in programs just like this called www.ResultsBreakthrough.com. All my own PowerTribe client get full use of this system at no cost for the first year.

4. MID-COURSE PROCESSES BRANCH

As your students are humming through that first pilot course, "things" will come up. Things that are unexpected always occur, and I consider them a gift. Because we are in our Pilot Program mode, we are looking for actions we can take to make the process run more smoothly as we scale the program. I assure you, if nothing comes up, I get worried. As good as I am at doing this, there's always a wrinkle that shows up, and we solve it quickly before it gets multiplied by the hundreds.

Let's review: Your Pilot has launched, you are running a dozen or so students through the process, and you are so far happy with the progress. During the pilot, I recommend a minimum of one weekly group coaching call and an extra day where we reserve a few hours at an odd time for "open office hours," where anyone can call with an immediate problem. In every interaction, request suggestions for improving the program – you won't get many, but you may get some great ones.

The other tool I like to suggest using is the surprise check-in. Pick a student who is doing well and another who is falling behind and make a friendly call to check in and see where they are at. Don't be shy, for they will appreciate the contact and may share with you a "golden nugget" of great information.

There's one more "secret weapon" we have in our tracking arsenal: the ability to watch digitally over our student's path as they progress through their program. Yes, you can set up the LMS environment to show you real time usage of the course and the pace at which students are moving through it. If someone doesn't show up for a few days (or any time frame you set), the system can nudge them to get back to their studies. The system will also notify you for that same reason.

You will be able to monitor which elements of the course are difficult for your students, and which ones your students are flying through. It's all part of the process of tracking the progress of your students.

As a reminder, you want your students to graduate and be successful even more than they do. They are struggling with the same self-talk and head trash that many people face when starting something new. Our job as leaders is to get them past all that and keep them plugging away. Never give up on your students, and they will thank you for it again and again!

5. END OF COURSE BRANCH

You are in the home stretch: your program is starting to mint new coaches/consultants as they finish up their training. You are not yet done, but you are getting close to the finish line. Let's use the end of the formal training to let them know about the soft skills they need to have, such as how to approach a new client, how to show up at a busy office, and how to act like a professional.

Another one of the secret weapons my Timeslips Certified Consultant Program had was a series of very friendly, well-written "lessons" about hygiene and appearance. I did this because my consultants were traveling to office environments to train lawyers and legal secretaries on how to use our software. To my shock and surprise, I realized I needed to make sure our CCs knew how not to look like Elmer Fudd when they showed up.

So, we brought in a wonderful writer who crafted some of the cutest bulletins and write-ups about how a professional should dress. It was light-hearted and complimentary; everyone loved reading them. If your CCs are not showing up in offices, then setting up expected guidelines about their promptness, political correctness, and attitude will set the stage for how they must act to stay in the program.

Use your ending modules to reinforce key values of the company, making sure they know how to talk about the company and your core mission; remind them of their obligations to protect the trademarks and copyrights of the company. Remind them of the promise the company has made to them, which is to deliver outstanding content that will prove to be extremely valuable.

As the CEO, you should help your PowerTribe fully understand exactly how you expect your CCs to behave. Make sure you reinforce your vision of what you want to accomplish with the company, in your life, and why they are there.

Later, at our annual Certified Consultant Symposium, we had some fun by reading aloud some of the complaints about our CCs dressing habits. One law firm sent me a letter complimenting the abilities of our CC but asked that we buy him a pair of pants! It was a great way to share our stories and reinforce our values at the same time.

Now it's time to ring the bell and graduate those lucky people who took a risk, trusted you, and signed up to be part of your Program. We have a lot in store for them.

Here are a few suggestions for activities with which you can finalize your new CC's graduation. These are all suggestions, and I would take them as such; I enjoy doing all of these, but you can decide which work best for you.

I recommend a printed and dated certificate with an expiration date that you have framed and prepared in a nice shipping container. It's the credential your new CC has worked hard to achieve. Now, let's make sure we are as proud of them as they are excited about this new opportunity. Send them their certificate and something else – for example, a monogrammed case for their laptop, which I used to get at Lands' End. Also, create a custom logo they can place on their website but remember to list the dates from when they are certified to when that certification expires, so they will need to renew every year.

Also, I would suggest you print a batch of business cards, co-branded with the company logo and the name of the Certified Consultant. This accomplishes two important things: it controls how your trademark is being used, AND it provides instant credibility for your CC along with limiting the credential issued to just one year, as mentioned above.

If you want to blow your new CCs away, create a branded custom template website where new CCs get their own website, of which you control the content. You can make it free for the first 90 days and then charge a small fee to maintain it. It's not unreasonable to charge $299 - $599 a year for a functional website, and if you multiply that by the number of CCs in your program a few years from now, the profits from that alone could pay an internal salary with ease. Remember, you can also SEO those sites individually, as well as set up product sales pages for your CCs to offer your products and make a small markup.

Next, it would be a great idea to have a group communications system they are enrolled in when they graduate. I feel an unsupervised chat room is a bad idea for an internal/external program like this, but a Facebook private group or a Slack channel is an excellent idea if – and only if – you have someone who will monitor it constantly. Remember, all companies can have problems, and we're judged not by what they are, but by the way we deal with them.

This is a great opportunity to deal with CC problems in a public forum while also being as responsive as possible. Still, be firm about upholding your values and ethics.

If you followed my lead and created the Code of Ethics I mentioned earlier, then you can post it as a document in the group for all to review as needed. So many problems can be handled by sticking to the CC Code of Ethics.

The next thing to do as they graduate is to review some of the material you provided at the beginning of their experience. Make sure you remind them of their legal obligation to uphold and respect your trademark. Explain again how your reputation is the most valuable thing you have in this marketplace and help them honor your commitment to them by reminding them of this important concept.

Also, take the time to review once again how they make money. Run webinars that explain your compensation plan or your revenue splits, (remember to make it visual and detailed); then record your webinar and put it inside your learning center as part of the resources you provide after they graduate.

TEACHING TO SELL

One of the lessons I learned building both a large consulting team and a coaching team is that the type of people who gravitate to these programs love to help others. It's a rare coach who has professional sales training and knows how to close a sale. You have another excellent opportunity here to run an introductory sales course over several 60-90 minute sessions; these courses will teach your CCs how to best sell your product. Later, I will show you how to monetize that, as well. The important point here is that the training you provide will only help them sell your products and their service. What could be wrong with that?

Since we are on the topic of sales, make sure that your CCs have as many sales tools in their arsenal as possible. The more you can create for them, the more they (and you) will sell. Think about it: you can probably recycle a lot of your existing sales pages, webinars, teleseminars, and live stage presentations for your CCs to use. They will appreciate this effort and thank you for the help.

Remember when I said in my introductory chapter that you were about to see how you can create a free army of salespeople who will pay you for the privilege of selling your products? Now you get what I mean!

It's a wonderful world when we can use powerful business tactics to get what we want and benefit our CCs, clients, and customers, all at the same time. And remember, they are paying you for this privilege. Treat your CCs like gold and they will recognize how well you are taking care of them. They are special, and they'll feel that recognition all the way to the bank.

Also, keep in mind that you are enabling a person to earn more money, improving the quality of their lives, and immersing them into a like-minded group so they feel a part of something bigger than themselves. Isn't that better than figuring out just one more sales channel?

LET'S REVIEW:

You've built an application process, you've designed your screening process, and you are now ready to enroll new students into your program. You start enrolling by selling folks on what you are offering, and they now pass through these processes with success.

You have your CC contract in place, your lawyer has blessed it, and you are ready to start using it. You know exactly what happens mid-way through the course, and how you will interact with students; alternatively, you know how they will react to your training. Also, you've built in a lot of communication touch points, which aids you in constantly monitoring progress, process, and quality.

You've designed your "End of Course" process knowing that your graduates are now ready to begin. You have their certificates ready to go, you have their social media badges designed, and you have planned their path from finishing the course work to starting work.

All of these steps are planned in advance before starting to build your program. If you've gone this far, they are finally ready for the next step: building your entire system.

If you would like more information about this phase of your program, go to www.PowerTribesBook.com/plan.

CHAPTER FIVE

THE POWERTRIBES BLUEPRINT

S UMMARIZING THE PROCESS.
In the learning stage, it's all about what is possible with a PowerTribe. My job is to make the benefits of a PowerTribe so clear that you will want to go out and build your own. In this learning phase, remember the three questions I posted earlier in the book about IF you are in a position to have an incredible launch and follow-through program.

These are the 3 critical questions I mentioned at the beginning of the book. For your convenience, here they are again:

1. Do you have a process, product or a device that causes a transformation or can deliver a high-value benefit to your client?

2. Is the process repeatable, and can it be taught to others who can then generate the same results? Or does this device need to be installed or configured to work perfectly?

3. Do you have a client base with enough potential students to make this all worthwhile?

If you answered yes to all three questions, then you have the opportunity to build something durable that can continuously generate cash into your company with very little overhead and support.

Phase One: The Strategy Phase

This is where most people get stuck; they are either not sure if they have the right type of company (go back to Phase Zero and ask yourself the three questions again), or they realize that it requires a time commitment and some focused effort.

It is in Phase One that all the planning and strategy you do sets up your success for the future phases. It is in Phase One that you organize your content and your Intellectual Property, or at least know where it is and what you have available.

As you read above, when I run a Phase One program, my goal is to have my clients fully aware of everything they will need to have a complete program. I've never lost anyone in Phase One, but if a client is not clear on their sales and up-sell processes, it takes longer. The good news is that if they are not clear before, they are perfectly clear by the end of Phase One.

If you've skipped the chapter called "Mapping Out Your Plan," then go back and read that first. It's more detailed and explains more about the process, whereas this chapter is a literal blueprint for your program.

You are planning every aspect of your program. Leave nothing out and the process of building it will be far easier for you and your staff. Let's start by naming your assets:

THE LEARNING MANAGEMENT SYSTEM:

There is a full chapter on your LMS, so this is an overview to help you see where it fits into the big picture. There are many LMS systems to choose from, and at different price points based on the type of services you want and need. I have selected the best LMS at the best price to build out the training for a PowerTribes "university" where you can house your entire system. The best way to get started is through my affiliate link, which will give you free access to build your entire program no matter how long it takes. It will also provide you with 5 "students" or staff members who can test your content as it is developed. By using my link, I get a tiny share of your enrollment when you do start paying; but more importantly, I get influence into the future direction of the company and the product. Either way, this is the best system to use: http://tiny.cc/mitch.

If you do choose to sign up for this service, send me a message at mitch@mitchrusso.com, and I will send you a link to the training video I made to get you started quickly.

When you build your course, it's best to break it up into three sections: Product Training, Systems Training, and "Back-End" Training – and then your Congratulations Module.

Product Training is where you train your new student on how to create the same effect as you do when you deploy your process or technology. It's a combination of taking them through your program as if they had purchased it as an end user would, and teaching them how to take others through your program. Both are included, and both are required.

For those people who you recruit out of your existing user/client group, you would then create a refresher course and focus more on the implementation aspect of your content. My suggestion is NOT to take an existing client through the basic training if they are already trained and have received the end result you sold when you first offered your program.

Systems Training is where you will train people how to use your internal systems. As part of many PowerTribes, Certified Consultants need to know how to access their portal to get to the "PowerTribes Only" sign-in. This is where you can post additional training materials, video presentations, downloads they can use with clients, and other information and documents you will need to share.

Back-End Training is only for those who build a "back end" for their Certified Consultants. A back-end system is where you create software that resides on a password protected portion of your website, to make your Certified Consultant's engagement go smoothly and easily. It's customized for use as a powerful tool set to speed the engagement and get results much faster when your CC is using the back end.

One of my clients had a process for rapidly building connections on LinkedIn. When we first started talking about their program, they didn't have any custom software to help their Certified Consultants, so I requested they build one. They did, and it's so powerful that now their internal staff use it for their own client engagements.

The value of a back-end system cannot be overemphasized. By having one, you help your CCs stay in your program longer, year after year. If they no longer stay certified, they lose access to this valuable tool that can automate and facilitate large parts of how they service clients. Can you understand why I asked them to build this?

Congratulations Module is where you award provisional certification and explain what to expect next. It is also a great place to continue building a personal relationship with your members by sharing stories, sharing your "why" stories in particular – and by welcoming them into the family.

Next comes your list of videos you need to record for your training environment. I suggest using a spreadsheet/map to organize your videos. On your spreadsheet, you can create the entire flow of your training system and then start to fill in the module names, the test questions you will use, and even the beginnings of a script.

A Short List of Video Categories:

» **Intro Video:** Welcome to the program.

» **Code of Ethics Review:** This is where you step through your code of ethics point by point, so it's perfectly clear where you stand.

» **The Contract Review Video:** This is where you go over the contract in detail, explaining exactly what they are getting, what their rights are, and what you expect from them. Remind them several times to review the contract with their own attorney before signing, to be safe.

» **Videos Required for Your Launch** (discussed in greater detail in other chapters):

  o Video One: The Shift/Disruption

  o Video Two: The Solution Emerging

  o Video Three: The Business Opportunity

Your Graduation and Congratulations Video: This will be a multi-part series where you also review many aspects of what comes after graduation. You will want to explain how client engagements work, how they can work with the company to close a lead, how to use the sales pages to sell their services and more.

NEXT, YOUR EMAIL CAMPAIGNS

In Phase One, you will plan your launch. If you are going to use an email and video launch, then you will need to sequence the launch emails and videos for maximum impact. You can use one of several products; Infusionsoft works great for this application.

When I work with a client, we generate about 40 emails that are used to move people through the process from start to finish, from prospect to post-graduation. Those emails are an asset that will need to be created as you build your sequence inside Infusionsoft.

If you email me and ask me for the email sequence list, I will send it to you. Mitch@mitchrusso.com

SALES SCRIPTS

After prospects watch your launch video sequence, they generally go to the application page, fill out the application, and use a credit card to prove they are really interested. If they don't qualify, they get their $100 back. The application needs to screen them to ensure they are a fit.

We develop a sales script for each client so that we know we are covering the key points of closing this type of sale. This is referred to as a "take away" sale. We call it that because we are taking away the opportunity to purchase if they don't qualify. It should motivate action toward us while we are moving away. Using urgency as part of the process, we have a high closing rate if the candidates are of excellent quality.

SALES TRAINING

There are two different types of sales training I recommend when building your program. The first is for your internal people who are closing sales from your application interviews. Those sales are critical, and training will be needed to ensure a high closing rate. The second type of sales training is for your graduate Certified Consultants. They will need training on how to close a sale for your product and their service. This is obviously the longer of the training programs you will need to develop, but it's a very natural process for any good sales executive to assist with, since it's part of how they already sell.

YOUR KEY DOCUMENTS:

I've mentioned these before; you will need three key documents to build and run your program. These documents will keep you safe, establish a baseline for behavior, and help define what your students get and don't get as part of what they pay for.

THE VENDOR AGREEMENT:

I learned the hard way while building my last company, that hiring Independent Contractors is an invitation to an audit; or at the very least, an unemployment insurance claim. When an independent contractor is let go for any reason, many will try to file for unemployment. As soon as they do that, you get an unemployment claim. You then have to explain to the state taxing authorities that that person was not an employee. Then the state can choose to prove they were an employee and claim that you owe back taxes, and possibly penalties for not paying said taxes on time.

Here's the solution: make sure that anyone you hire has a Federal ID number, proving that they are an independent company. Then, when you sign your contract with them, you are contracting with a company, not a person. Later, as you create lead flow for your CCs, you can then share their consulting fees with them, through their company. NOTE: Check all of this with your accountant and attorney before you create or sign any contract.

THE COACHING CODE OF ETHICS:

I've brought this up on several occasions; it's the governing laws of your tribe. If these are well crafted, then you will have a group that totally understands exactly how the culture is set. Remember, you create the culture for your tribe; never let the tribe create a culture, because that will backfire and no one will win.

THE FRANCHISE QUESTIONNAIRE:

This is an optional document that I highly recommend in order to stay as clear of franchise law as possible. Franchise law is different for every state; some states don't have many restrictions or conditional obligations at all. Here's why I think you need The Franchise Questionnaire: it is a detailed questionnaire that YOU fill out and share with your new CCs. It answers every question that a new franchisee should ask and clearly explains the risk, the opportunity, the expenses, and the chances of success or failure. By having this document signed by every Certified Consultant, proving that they have read it, understand it, and received it, most states will leave you completely alone if there's an inquiry. Of course, I cannot guarantee the future actions of anyone or any government body, but this is an excellent precaution and worth the trouble.

THE SOFTWARE SYSTEMS YOU CAN USE TO RUN YOUR POWERTRIBE:

I've already mentioned the LMS software above. Here's the rest of what you will need:

CRM FOR SUPPLYING LEADS TO YOUR POWERTRIBE:

Lead flow is the lifeblood of your tribe; it's what sets you apart from any other coaching or training certification and will cause your CCs to stay certified at additional fees year after year. You will need a CRM system to manage the lead flow and ensure all your Certified Consultants are receiving their fair share of leads.

We like to use Zoho CRM (www.Zoho.com) because it will allow us to reclaim leads that are not followed up on in a specific period of time. Not all CRM systems do this. It's easy to use, it's inexpensive, and it can be integrated into your back-end portal for your CCs to access.

CUSTOMER SERVICE AND SUPPORT:

Depending on the size of the program you are building, you may want a trouble ticket system. This is a SaaS platform that allows CCs to enter a trouble ticket or a question directly into a specialized database so their questions will reach the right person inside your organization for an answer.

What I like best about using a system like this is that for every answer you provide to every question that is posted, the system builds a knowledge base of your answers. Next time someone asks the same or a similar question, it will show them the likely solution and save your company from needing to spend the time answering that same question yet again.

The two systems that I am most familiar with are www.ZenDesk.com and www.FreshDesk.com, both of which are inexpensive and easy to use. Take a look at both, and if you think you are going have more than fifty people in your PowerTribe, it may make sense to start using a system to track your service needs.

Another useful system is Camtasia, a screen recording software that is very valuable in creating professional training lessons. Using PowerPoint or any slide builder, you simply speak into a microphone as you are running your slides in real time, and Camtasia records the whole session. Besides recording, Camtasia has powerful editing tools and makes the process very easy. You can learn more by following this link: http://techsmith.com/camtasia

BUILDING YOUR NEW BUSINESS MODEL:

This part may be the most important work you do to determine the future value of your PowerTribe to your company. This is the strategy element of building your framework.

Start with the following questions:

» Where do clients come from? - List all current sources.

» What is your selling process? - Map this out for each channel: online, phone, trade show, in person, etc.

» What are the key elements of your closing conversation? - List the talking points of a successful close or, if online, list the promises you make and benefits you deliver, and show each for every product or service.

After you've constructed this in a mind map or a spreadsheet, ask yourself exactly how having a Certified Consultant could enhance or upgrade that sale. Find out why people didn't buy in the past and ask yourself, "If I would have included two to four free coaching sessions, would that make the sale more compelling, and how much more could I close?"

Your Certified Consultants will be hungry to get started and build client relationships. If you give them the opportunity to meet with a client repeatedly, in order to build a relationship and prove their value, don't you think they would jump at the chance to take those free sessions? You bet they would. These are the most qualified leads they will ever get.

THE POWERTRIBE BENEFIT SUMMARY:

» CCs get live, fresh leads by helping clients for free for a limited number of sessions.

» The company gets to set a higher value on their standard offering with free coaching sessions.

» Both the company and the CC now have a selling opportunity that neither one had before.

You can use this to revive your old prospects who never bought, find new clients who would have never considered your services without the free coaching, and, when the coaching services are sold after the free time runs out, your company can get a percentage of the revenue charged for that coaching/consulting service.

This is part of your planning. Look carefully at the spreadsheet or mind map after you have constructed it and see exactly where a high-powered Certified Consultant can be used to grow the business.

Another example: trade shows and public events. Invite your CCs and let them offer their services free to anyone who buys your offering. Once again, it's a win-win across the board.

What else can we do now that we have a multi-hundred coaching/consulting organization at our disposal?

Let's tackle competitors. Do they have a national network in every state, and can they summon a half-dozen people to show up at any regional meeting in 48 hours? One thing is for sure: you do! Now, what can you do with this new superpower? Think about all the ways you can mutually benefit the company and your PowerTribe.

In Phase Two, you create everything you designed in Phase One: you bring all your intellectual property – your training videos, lectures, live teaching recordings, etc. – along with anything else we need to take a new student through to the end of the learning cycle. If you are doing this on your own, make a list of everything you have. Then break up the content into the four groups I talked about earlier and start sequencing the order of your presentation.

All of Phase Two is about building your internal systems. Besides populating the LMS with your content, you will also need the entire launch sequence built: all the videos and emails, sales pages, CRM screens your CCs will use for tracking, what you want to track, and everything else you need to run your program. These things must be built from scratch to conform fully to the needs of your program.

BLUEPRINTING PHASE TWO:

Phase Two starts when Phase One is done. You've now created the master plan: you've figured out what your infrastructure will look like, and you've identified your Program Manager and the software tools you will need to deploy. The next step is the hardest: building out your plan.

I recommend three outside vendors to help you if you don't already have the type of staff you need for the following tasks.

Vendor #1: Get an Infusionsoft consultant and let them build of all the back-end management and infrastructure you will need to orchestrate the dozens of moving parts required to get people enrolled, completed, and graduated.

Vendor #2: Find a great copywriter who can write all 40+ emails that will be sent through Infusionsoft. If you have this capability, then they will be busy for weeks on this task. NOTE: Many of the emails are mundane and simple, like, "Your credit card did not go through, please resubmit using a different card," which may even be pre-populated and can be tweaked. But your sales page and your video scripts will require someone with skills.

Vendor #3: Your CRM consultant. As I mentioned above, we use Zoho, and it's fairly easy to use. But a good Zoho consultant can really make this system handle a higher level of management, such as knowing when leads are not followed up on, shifting those leads to a different person, and monitoring the state of each lead as it goes through the sales process.

Once you have these three skill sets lined up, the next big thing will be to build out the Learning Management System (LMS) content. These are your lessons. I covered this earlier in the book, but I am also naming it here in the blueprint section as part of your process.

Phase Two is over when you have battle-tested every element of the launch and confirmed that it works flawlessly. Then you launch your program. This is Phase Three.

Imagine if you were Noah and you knew the floods were coming. You build this huge vessel, the Ark, to take two of every species to safety until the flood waters recede. While out there in the weather, you have no access to anything other than what you brought with you. While building and stocking the Ark, you would have to figure out what every animal would eat, where they would defecate, where to put them so they wouldn't eat each other, how they can get fresh air into the Ark so no one would die of the odor, and how to store enough fresh water.

All the work outlined above must be done before the Ark is launched.

All of your materials for your launch have to be prepared with the same high level of certainty, because once your student graduates and is working with clients, it's much harder to call them back in for more training when you realized you missed something important.

Just stay fully involved and give this your all. If you do this work as best as you can up front it will pay off in a colossal way.

PHASE THREE BEGINS WHEN YOU LAUNCH.

Now the fun starts.

The videos are sequenced out; the application finally goes live and leads start flooding in. Your sales team is busy making qualifying calls, and within hours the "bell rings" and your first sale is made.

Wow, $20K, one sign-up, and there's one hundred applications still to call; two hundred, three, they're streaming in now. Things are starting to get of fun. Less than a week goes by, and you've closed your pilot enrollment at twenty people and have $300K in the bank and another $100K+ coming in on payment plans.

Now the real work starts: getting those 20 people to become successful at deploying your system, using your tools, and getting the same great results YOU get when you are delivering your transformational product/service.

Now is when you are paying close attention, monitoring every student and watching to see who gets stuck and where. When the LMS alerts you that one of your students hasn't shown up for three days, your program manager starts calling and emailing: "Where are you? What's going on? What problems are you having?" And you get that person back on track.

Your attitude must be: "Their Success is MY Responsibility." And if you hold to that, you will get most people through.

Somewhere between 30 and 90 days later, you will be graduating your students and getting them leads. Monitor this process carefully. Make sure they are handling prospect calls with the same respect and quality of training you would like yourself. Make as many mid-course corrections as you can. It's your job to make them successful. And when they are successful, you get...

Testimonials! Your testimonials will be used to enroll the next class. Send out a videographer to the clients' homes or offices and professionally video each testimonial. Create a testimonial guide that helps your students record the perfect testimonial according to your recipe. You can find local videographers on Craigslist.org for about $100 a visit. Some will even handle post-production for you, too.

Now that you have gotten your CCs successfully selling and earning, your company has evolved to the next plane of existence. You will soon, within one year, have a hundred or more Certified Consultants representing your company and making a great living while evolving into a big, beautiful new sales channel.

It should take about 90 days from start to finish. If it takes much longer, then something is wrong, and the problem needs to be diagnosed. Your job as the CEO is to manage this process and eliminate the roadblocks as they appear.

Are you up for the task of creating the next big thing for your company?

For a download of the entire blueprint, go to www.PowerTribesBook.com/blueprint

CHAPTER SIX

THE LEARNING MANAGEMENT SYSTEM

THE LEARNING MANAGEMENT SYSTEM

I F YOU ARE OVER 40, you may remember your first week of employment when you were positioned in front of a VCR to watch training videos. When I started work at Digital Equipment Corp. many years ago, I spent two weeks watching endless hours of videos.

I don't know about you, but I daydreamed during some of those videos. I know others who went to the bathroom while the VCR was running. Let's agree that video training is not particularly effective at teaching concepts that require mastery.

The reason? Because streaming videos for longer than 15 minutes usually conveys too many "facts" and concepts without a way to test the employee's skills and discover if they really fully understand. This one fact has been the bane of training companies and training processes for decades.

When I designed the Virtual Training Environment with Tony Robbins, I worked with world-class experts who perfected the art of helping people learn efficiently and quickly. While working with Tony, I discovered what was missing from most training programs, and I participated in the construction of this material to create a comprehensive, impactful learning environment.

The reason this is so critical is that without full comprehension, we can't trust our clients in the hands of our Certified Consultants or coaches. That is a disaster waiting to happen, as I found out first hand when my first class of Certified Consultants was dispatched to client sites only to create a wave of problems for the company to solve.

This is what I do for my clients when we work together on their PowerTribe: I ensure their new Certified Consultants are trained to 100% comprehension using a series of interlocking lessons, quizzes, tests, and application of the material.

THE SECRET OF A GREAT TRAINING PROGRAM

It's in the nuance of how you check for full comprehension. There are three basic steps which, when applied correctly, can almost guarantee 100% understanding after the course is complete.

» Never "teach" through video for more than 12 – 15 minutes at a time; shorter times are better than longer times.

» At the end of each lesson, write a short quiz that checks to see if your students understood their teachings, and make sure that it is both informative and entertaining.

» Your quiz should be a learning tool as well as an assessment tool. This means that the quiz should convey valuable information throughout the process of discovering if they know the right answers.

» Application is key. Many people take quizzes so they can pass a test; they may know the answers and pass the test, but can they apply the material? That's the difference that creates competence.

» After several lessons related to the same overall sub-section of your material (we will call it a module in a syllabus for this discussion), test again.

» Use a variety of testing options: ask questions, require essays, use multiple choice, and use direct answers in the form of "free-form answers" to your questions.

» Demonstration is a form of proof of concept. Use pictures and video to demonstrate a concept, and then ask your students to sketch the sequence, which is a stronger proof-set than just answering questions. If sketching is a challenge, then find another way for students to prove to you they can apply what they are being taught.

» If your material is lengthy, allow for some human interaction and stop the process long enough to require a live (or on-screen) presentation from your students on what they have learned and how they see it working in the real world.

» Break up the training with live Q&A sessions, group coaching, and check-in calls. Don't ask students to study and test continuously without giving them a chance to apply the material.

» If you can build in interaction, this heightens the experience and adds to comprehension. Always allow for your students to ask questions at every stage of the process.

» This is an excellent place to introduce accountability partnerships as I mentioned earlier in the book, using my system designed exactly for this purpose can be found at http://www.resultsbreakthrough.com/. Inside, you can create specific accountability questions for each module.

» If you are training Certified Consultants on how to use software, make the software available to them so they can practice along with their lessons. Teach students how to capture live screens and ask them for proof they completed the task at hand.

This is just the beginning of what it takes, but if you read this one short section and abide by the rules I've explained here, your material will be understood at a far higher level than if you had simply charged ahead and created a course.

Having your course is a great first step, but it does not complete your task, which is getting ready for your first pilot launch. Just because you have educated your new candidates doesn't mean they know how to behave or appear professional, either in person, live, or on the phone. It's a good idea to create a new set of lessons or modules that instruct them how to behave like a professional, just as I did at Timeslips Corp. Then introduce problem-handling role-play to ensure they can maintain the integrity of your relationship with clients.

Let's call this "finishing school" for your graduates! It must be done with care and sensitivity, so no one is offended in the process. You are not telling your CCs that you think they can't handle being professional; you are simply ensuring that they act as you and your company would when dealing with clients.

This simple step makes sure your CCs are not walking into a client's office dressed for the beach, or smelling like last night's dinner, or starting calls late. It's important to stress what professional standards you have set for yourself, your staff, and now your new Certified Consultants.

I hope that by now you see the value of building a robust, complete training environment that you can use with confidence, and that you start to scale your operation. It will serve you well for many years to come.

This same system can be used internally to train new staff as they join the company. How many times has one person left the company and impacted the operation in a negative way? Using the Learning Management System to encapsulate the knowledge of each job or position in the company could save you from a future disaster and eliminate overdependence on one single individual.

USE TRACKING TECHNOLOGY TO KEEP EVERYONE ENGAGED.

Most of the more comprehensive learning management systems have tools built-in to track student progress. The tools are there, but you have to know what you want to monitor before you start fiddling with the controls.

I suggest setting up a framework for constant monitoring of their progress through your course. Find out what they are struggling with, what problems they have or perceive they may have, and/or where they are not fully clear on the material itself.

What you are looking for is making sure they are not rushing through the course at too steep a gradient or moving on past a point of confusion. Some people are quite adept at "studying" like they did in college, just to pass the test and not for practical application. Don't let that person slip through.

Learning Management Systems, if used to their full advantage, can ensure 100% comprehension. This is a bold claim, but it can be proven to work by following the steps I explained above: short, succinct groups of material followed by a short quiz designed to test their knowledge and their ability to apply.

DIFFERENT TYPES OF LEARNING MANAGEMENT SYSTEMS

Just like most software categories, there are many to choose from. Some are very expensive and come with a team of advisors behind that five-figure price; some are free, but most have a monthly charge. There are several that have a one-time cost and operate as plug-ins for WordPress. Even those can be very powerful but depend on your website to be available to students. This will be a quick review of Learning Management Types and then some examples.

VIRTUAL TRAINING ENVIRONMENTS

In a virtual training environment, the student is immersed in a two-dimensional presentation of a three-dimensional space. Much like the HoloDeck on Star Trek, you are watching and interacting with people who appear to be live on your screen, directing you through the learning material. You are presented with live pie charts and graphs where you, as the student, can change the numbers and watch the graphics change, as well. Furthermore, you can ask questions and, in several cases, have the software respond to your questions with a video of a live person telling you the answer.

Virtual Training Environments are the top of the food chain when it comes to Automated Training Environments, but they come with a substantial price. In many cases, the cost to produce live courseware costs about $5,000 an hour of finished material. If you can afford the time and the money, usually in the range of several hundred thousand dollars, then that's hands-down the best way to go. It does take many months to complete, so be prepared.

The leader in this industry is www.LightSpeedVT.com, which was the partner I worked with to create Tony Robbins's virtual training course back in 2011. The results were spectacular, but it took months and months to get the finished product.

A different approach is a hosted, interactive solution. Some of the best training is housed in systems like this. While not "virtual" with live video simulating a human relationship, the hosted interactive solution can be very cost effective and deliver powerful results. There are many on the market, and I have done extensive research to discover which is best for the type of programs I build with my clients.

Maybe you've heard of www.Kajabi.com; it is a course-building platform and is very popular. Some big-time trainers use it to store and spool out their material. In my opinion, it is little more than a VCR on the Internet. Yes, it can house your videos and downloads, but it doesn't have the tools we need to assess, track, and graduate students. It's basic, and for some people, it is perfect the way it is. But not for us.

NOTE: As this is going to press, a new version of Kajabi appears to have many new additional features, which may make it a good choice for your program.

Here's what we are looking for: we want the ability to present any content we have now or may have in the future. We want our system to know when a student doesn't fully "get" the content, and, if they can't master it, can send them back to restudy.

We also want a system that keeps track of what's going on inside our student population, and which will let us know when someone is falling behind. The system should be able to let the student know when they are falling behind and send notices that they need to get back to work. In addition, we need a platform that can work on phones, tablets, desktop, Mac, or PC – virtually anything that can display a web browser.

Finally, it has to be inexpensive. There are several that cost very little for a few students, but rapidly get into the range of hundreds of dollars per month.

MY FAVORITE PROGRAM

I am sure there are many that qualify, but the one I select most of the time for my client is TalentLMS: http://tiny.cc/mitch.

This fits all of my qualifications for a near-perfect system, and it's getting better all the time. If you are already using one of the other systems for a different reason, then consider switching, because this product has everything most people need. You can even launch courses from it directly and sell your courses through their e-commerce front end.

Whichever one you choose, don't try to certify your clients without an LMS, or you will likely fail trying. I've seen 3-day classes where several hundred people jam into an auditorium. Then, an instructor runs endlessly through days' worth of material. At the end of those three days, you are "certified" and get your certificate. Would you trust your clients to be served by people trained that way?

Once you've selected the specific LMS system you want to use, it's time to build your training plan.

Your LMS training program is made up of lessons. These are followed by quizzes, which are grouped together into sections covering one specific topic. Those topics can be grouped together into modules, which have an overall subject or purpose. In turn, a group of modules is considered a "track" your students will follow on their path to graduating. In your LMS, there are at least three tracks, which we will review.

Each lesson must build on the previous one; never skip around when creating your Certification training system. Use the ideas and concepts from the previous lesson to build upon in the next one. Sequencing is important, so carefully plan your program.

Build a map of each lesson, module, and content, so you will know before you begin creating your system what you are trying to accomplish. This outline will be your guide as you build your system.

Track 1: Orientation. The first lesson is about the market within which your CCs will be working. It's important to provide an overview from the company's perspective and where they fit into the market. The next lesson should be about the values of the company – the vision of the founder and the goals for the following years. This aligns your new CCs with the company right away and makes sure they understand why you are doing what you do. The next lesson can be an overview of the Code of Ethics. This is a great way to make sure that all new CCs understand what your standards are of right and wrong, how to treat our IP, and how to treat each other.

Tell stories about how the culture of your company is supportive, ethical, and caring. Use this precious time to open their hearts so they will let you in, while you do the same for them. You have not just built a company, but a family! Your expression of caring and appreciation should now be obvious. Invite them in to see just who you are and why you are here. Show them that you want the same things they do: a great life, a lot of love, attention, and success in their work.

Track 2: Product Training. This is a fully self-contained course built for 100% comprehension and is designed to take a student from start to finish through all the product training. At the end of this track, your students will have covered all aspects of the course well enough to use the product themselves. It may occur to you that you could potentially sell this course to new clients. We can look at that later, but yes, it's a possibility, as long as it doesn't set up cross-purposes with our CC program graduates.

Track 2 will be the longest and most in-depth part of the program. It's going to be important to first break up your material into modules that cover specific topics. Second, each module must be planned in advance to cover all of the material you will need for your student to fully comprehend it. In Track 2, you will be planning this training in a similar way to how you might train someone sitting by your side. Think that way when you start planning your modules.

Track 3: Internal Systems Training. This is where you show your students how to enter new clients into your system, how to find existing clients, and how to look up their activity. The internal system training will also cover the custom application, which I highly suggest you create to help your CCs perform their work with clients.

The goal of this custom application is to make your company "sticky," so if CCs want to do this type of work, they will want your company to facilitate the technology back-end; in turn, this makes their work go more smoothly. I also advocate a CRM system set-up just for CCs, so that they can take detailed notes on every client interaction. Your CRM system also keeps an accurate account of all emails sent to clients, which you can inspect anytime you want.

The CRM system also shows which CCs are generating the most activity, and it should be used to monitor their actions. While we are not creating a "big brother" atmosphere, we are making our CCs aware that we will be looking into their activity to protect the integrity of our company's brand and reputation, as well as protecting them from doing something wrong.

Track 4: "Congratulations" and Next Step Module. Use your ending modules to reinforce fundamental values of the company, making sure your CCs know how to talk about the company and your core mission. Remind them of their obligations to protect the trademarks and copyrights of the company, and of the promise the company has made to them, which is to deliver outstanding content that will prove to be precious. As the CEO, you should help your PowerTribe fully understand exactly how you expect your CCs to behave. Make sure you reinforce your vision of what you want to accomplish with this company in your life, and why they are there.

GETTING READY TO BUILD YOUR TRAINING PLATFORM

Start collecting as much information as you need to train someone in your field, practice, or process, just as if you were sitting next to them and walking them through it. It would be excellent if you could train everyone yourself, just so that you could ensure they learn from the person in the company most qualified for training new people, but this is almost impossible. Gather your PowerPoint presentations, Word documents, videos, graphics, charts, graphs, phone calls, interviews – everything you could or would use to ensure someone is fully trained.

Many years ago, I used to pay my staff members a bonus if they were to create a full training manual for the job they were doing. This served two important functions: it allowed me to make the person who was doing the job replaceable, so that if they ever left the company, it would be easy to replace them. The other reason was that it provided me with a roadmap on how they assimilate information – how they learn. I realized back then that we all learn differently. Some prefer more visual presentations, others more audible content, and still others prefer to read and learn.

This set the stage for how I like to organize the material that I need to train a new staff member, employee, or vendor.

If you organize your information in the exact sequence as you would present it if you were training someone live in your office, then you can ensure that your CCs will understand what you are teaching them with the same effectiveness. Then, making sure it is as complete as it can be, get someone in your organization to run through the material to make sure they can "get it" with just only minimal guidance from you.

Although it's important to ensure your material is understandable on its own, direct guidance is also helpful. If you were sitting next to your Consultant, you would perform a practice or do something specific, and then you would check in with that person as they watched/listened to what you did. It's important to ask, "Did you see what I did there?" or "Did you understand why I did or said that?" Essentially, we are mirroring this learning process using all the same content we might use if we were training everyone ourselves. The big difference between a stack of old videos and a well-designed LMS comes down to two essential ideas: use very small amounts of information at a time, and then test carefully and thoughtfully for comprehension.

Now that you know about small chunks of information, organize your material the same way. Start with your introductory material and break it up into very consumable pieces, about 4 – 6 minutes per chunk (longer if need be to explain a single concept fully, but still as short as possible), and write a short quiz for each chunk.

Use as many questions as you must, ensuring that each quiz checks the most important elements of the last piece you wanted your student to learn. As you accumulate chunks and exams, start to build modules from these as a group. As a reminder, use your questions to reinforce the lessons they just reviewed.

MAKING SURE YOU ARE ORGANIZED!

By organizing all the training material in advance, we can see what data belongs to which module or group of information.

Each module can cover something specific and relevant to the whole process, yet stand separately according to skill, concept, or operation. Then, create a "final exam" for each module, requiring an additional long essay on how they would apply the material.

Here's a tip for creating your modules: the first set of lessons must be the language, concepts, and nomenclature of your subject. This means you must define all of the words, technical terms, and any derivatives up front; make sure your student knows the definitions before they start their lessons. Test them for extra assurance.

When a person passes a misunderstood word, they can momentarily go blank and get a not-there feeling due to not understanding what they are reading or studying. If they don't stop and look up that misunderstood word, instead continuing to study, they will likely quit the course, or worse: force themselves through with a lot of misunderstood words, rendering the entire subject mostly useless to them. This makes your new students mostly useless to you. So, catch those misunderstood words up front before they get too far down the road, when it will be much more difficult to recover them.

HERE'S HOW TO DO IT, AND I BELIEVE THIS IS THE SECRET TO A GREAT COURSE.

Start by defining all the words and the concepts up front. Include technical words, industry jargon, slang, and, of course, common words used in specialized ways. Then create well-crafted definitions that apply directly to your product, company, and industry.

Now, present several words and definitions grouped together at a time, and set up your quiz to ask your students to describe what those specific words or phrases mean in their own words. Afterward, request several sentences showing the context and meaning, along with how they may apply (if not completely obvious) to your subject or topic. Despite how long it may take, this will be the best time spent up front before you dive into your material. While it may seem odd to add additional time to your course, if done well and at the beginning, it will deliver more competent students faster than if you never did this.

Get your modules arranged by topic as we discussed above, then group modules together based on the flow of how your company works. This means starting with your introductory company information; let your first modules be about the founder, the mission of the founder (the "Why" of the founder,) and the vision of the company. Get your students excited to become part of something new and interesting to them; show that new person the picture of who you are and why they are there.

Finally, it's all about the culture of your program. No matter where your culture training sits in the arc of your training system, make sure your company culture is crystal clear to everyone who passes through your environment. I like to place the culture training on Track One so that students get oriented at the start and know what to expect. Like all of the material we offer to our Certified Consultants, the culture course must have an interactive quiz in order to pass through to the next section. The quiz reminds them of what we covered and makes sure that they understand how important culture is to our program. For my own clients, I provide the culture code and the entire training module ready to be recorded.

CHAPTER SEVEN

DELIBERATELY CREATE YOUR CULTURE

CREATING THE CULTURE OF YOUR TRIBE DELIBERATELY

WHAT IS CULTURE, ANYWAY? If you are the founder of a company, your values define the culture. It's the feeling people get when they work for your company or are associated with your company. Culture is basically three things:

1. How they feel being part of your culture.
2. What they can do to support your company and build their own life around it.
3. What they cannot do – what would be wrong, immoral, illegal, or not conforming with the "Why" of the CEO.

It's all about values, plain and simple. Many companies don't know how to create the value structure they need in order to have a great culture. That's what this chapter is all about: building the value set we are going to all live by as the company grows.

The people who join an organization want to identify what the culture is so that they can operate freely within that culture. At Zappos (online shoe store), the agents are empowered to do anything to please the client and make them feel good about calling Zappos. That's their culture, but maybe not what you want.

We are attracting professional people who have a set of needs, and we appeal to those needs when we show them what our program is all about. Who are these people?

In essence, there are three types of people who we observe show up as Certification clients:

1. They want Certification in order to be the best at what they do; this is who they are.
2. They want to earn more money with a proven program.
3. They want to be part of a community and love the involvement in a high-level group.

Our goal in building a Certification Program is to appeal to all three.

Your Certification Program will be far more efficiently than the one I first built in 1989 while adding several NEW revenue streams at the same time.

But before we get to the mechanics, you need to understand how this all weaves into the fabric of social structure and business.

More than you realize, you are about to create a group with a particular set of group dynamics. In effect, you are creating a new social structure, and how you create that group will determine if you succeed or fail. No other element of this program is more important than understanding the impact this group can have on those team members and your company.

THE REAL GENESIS OF A TRIBE.

In Seth Godin's book, *Tribes*, he makes some compelling observations. I want to quote him here so that we can set the stage for our next discussion:

"A Tribe is a group of people connected to one another, connected to a leader, and connected to an idea."

The "idea" or process is the most important thing, and the Tribe Leader is responsible for showing people how to create the same effect as the leader themselves creates.

So, how does this apply to what you are doing with your PowerTribe? Using the formula Seth constructed above, we will test our idea and see if it fits the concept of a tribe:

We want to form a group of people (who will become Certified Consultants) who are connected to each other (through Facebook groups and other electronic methods), connected to a leader (you and your company), and connected to an idea.

In this case, the idea is the Freedom to earn money in their own business and cause the same beautiful transformation in their clients as you have done with yours.

We will show you how your CCs can be free to use their knowledge and passion to help others, make money, and advance their lives. Their eventual goal: to earn a full-time living or be financially free, and, ultimately, to be part of something bigger that's purposeful as well as contributes to the lives of others.

The Tribes that Seth discusses in his book are all about creating passion around an important social cause or movement, alongside a polarized group of opinionated people who all feel the same way.

Our PowerTribe starts by attracting the top 5% of our client base, who are already using our products, technology, or services at the highest level of proficiency, to make money and be a part of something bigger.

They are the ones who will be most attracted to what we are about to offer. NOTE: They don't always have to be from your existing clients or customers; eventually, you will attract people outside your immediate circle. But for the first several waves of applicants, it's best to build your base with existing clients.

As I mentioned above, some percentage of your applicants who want to become a Certified Consultant are more interested in becoming experts, and never have any intention to offer their services to clients. Some companies will sponsor someone to take the training for internal support of existing staff. But the majority of applicants have a clear business objective, and they enter into the program with the primary goal to make money. After joining, they enjoy becoming part of the community and build bonds with those already there.

As we will soon realize, it's our job as leader of our PowerTribe to make sure we accommodate and facilitate team and community building with strong group communications systems.

What about an additional "test" to see if we are really building a Tribe?

Quoting from Seth's book:

1. The effectiveness of the tribe can be measured by how it transforms a shared interest in a passionate goal and a desire to change themselves and the world.
2. The Leader provides tools to members who create and then tighten communications.
3. Leadership then leverages the Tribe to allow it to grow and gain new members.

Let's once again see if we pass the test.

1. We are transforming several shared interests into passionate goals, which support both their self-improvement and the way business operates more efficiently.

2. As mentioned above, we create a very rich community environment for our Certified Consultants to share tips and tricks and become better acquainted.

3. This is where we excel as a Tribe. We leverage the power of the tribe by helping our Certified Consultants generate income, create their own client relationships, and attract more members as the success of our Tribe grows.

I think we passed. So why am I taking you through this process?

Because if I can show you that you are building a real tribe of human souls, then you will soon see how we can further leverage the psychological power of our natural desire to join and be part of a group that supports us individually.

For most people, being part of a group that leads members to where they want to be while also creating a profound and meaningful support environment is a rare experience. If that same group nurtures them in countless ways while creating bonds that normal companies can't accomplish even with their own employees, then you will have created something more valuable than any product or service and which will likely endure beyond the confines of this one company.

Even beyond making money, the collective genius can be used to help individual members as if they are in a mastermind experience. If every member is focused on the same overall goal as the sponsoring company, then they will have a deep feeling of belonging beyond any business arrangement or paid experience.

This is what we must accomplish if we want our group to thrive. In my own experience, several of the Certified Consultants who joined my Timeslips Certified Consultant Program during the late 1980's are still in touch with me for the very reasons I stated above.

CREATING THE COMMUNITY.

As I've illustrated above, a group that is isolated from each other and the company is bound to fail.

As the CEO of a company, you may be concerned about having an open group where people can express grievances. I have discovered that despite our concerns, with the right culture installed correctly, the group is self-correcting.

Here's what happens when you get a group of people together who are all dedicated to a common mission.

THEY HELP EACH OTHER!

Unbelievable as it may sound, they come together to support the company that sponsored them, as long as the company is coming from the right place and has proven they will sustain and protect the group. Community leaders will start to emerge; specific niche players will start to identify themselves as the leaders they naturally are. Others who want to help your company with their own services will show up, as well.

As this starts to happen, you are watching your community beginning to gel into a cohesive group, which has an attraction factor of its own.

Sooner or later, you are going to be presented with "the test;" if you fail, you will lose the respect of your members and could signal the decline of morale and enthusiasm in the group.

Here's the test:

Someone will emerge as a "bad seed" and start to badmouth others, the company, and/or the founders, and even try to gain support around their grievances.

If you let that happen – if you don't act quickly to cut them from the group or handle this diplomatically and with decisive action – you are dead meat. You've failed the test.

Everyone will be watching to see what you do. You will be telegraphing to the rest of the group what they can expect in the future; how much leeway they might have should they create a problem; or exactly what will happen when the next person acts up.

You must be decisive. You must act with courage and with grace. Your goal is NOT to embarrass the individual or hurt them in any way; it's to get them under control quickly.

As an example, we had one very intelligent man who joined our program and had many suggestions for improving our software, which we welcomed and acknowledged. But he complained about everything. Nothing was good enough for him; no one should enjoy the program if he didn't, and he made that clear.

Then at a public event, he stood up and told me what he wanted me to do with the program and how it should be run. In this public forum with several hundred CCs in the room, I responded with respect, but firmly. I said that I didn't think this program was a fit for him anymore, and I invited him to leave.

He was shocked! His "self-importance" was so high that he never dreamed I would let him go. But I did. I drew the line, firmly and publicly. I became quiet as I waited for his answer. He simply waved his hand like, "get outta here" and sat down.

Confrontation over. And from then on, when he spoke about how bad everything was, other CCs now echoed my words, "Maybe the program just isn't for you," and laughed.

Eventually, I had to call him privately and let him know that we would not renew his certification, and he was angry. I spent time explaining why, and he called me a dictator. Yes, I explained, it's my program, and I run it for the good of everyone involved, but I set the rules, and he clearly wasn't interested in following them. And so we parted, professionally, decisively, and with respect for the contribution he had made.

The other CCs watched carefully how I handled that. They now knew where the boundaries were drawn; it made it easy to understand what was expected and what wasn't.

Now let's deal with the opposite issue. Someone does something exceptionally well, and the company doesn't notice.

Here again, we need decisive action to recognize the individual and call them front and center to be seen and appreciated. The effect of this one action can generate dozens of similar positive actions over the course of the next year. Other Certified Consultants or coaches will seek to do something exceptional, just to be noticed, loved, and appreciated.

This is one part of what building a culture deliberately is all about.

Your culture dictates how your CCs will act and react. When you don't have a culture, you leave everything to chance and end up with entropy. Entropy is defined simplistically as chaos, disorganization, and randomness.

That's NOT a good thing. Instead, we want our culture to feel safe, structured, and very well-balanced.

If we substitute the word "family" instead of culture, it may make more sense. A family has parent(s): leaders of the family. So does a company, in the form of the management team. A family has rules; a family has events; and a family supports each other even when things are not going well. Obviously, a family paradigm has its limitations; we can't fire a family member, even though sometimes we may want to. We can fire a Certified Consultant from our program, and in time, it will happen.

All the characteristics we named above are very important when creating your CC culture. The more clear and concise you are about what you want your culture to be, the better and safer people will feel. The better and clearer the boundaries are set, the more comfortable your CC community members will feel.

The more parents pay attention to their kids, the better the kids will feel, in general. A great CC program has a strong leader, a well-defined code of ethics, and an inclusive and supportive culture.

It's your job to create that culture, and if you do, you will have one of the most resilient groups of fans, friends, and business partners in your industry.

A quick story about culture and the effect of a public action:

In most companies today, when it's someone's birthday, we get them a cake and call a short meeting in the conference room to celebrate. After the sugar rush starts to wear off, everyone is back to his or her desks. What would happen if someone's birthday were NOT celebrated the same way? That's "judgment," and that person will feel like no one likes him or her enough to have a birthday cake. Before long, that person will be resentful and angry. That's a ripple in the Matrix and can soon become a wave if not properly handled.

When I ran my Certified Consultant Program, we had one of our Consultants get sick – really sick. We knew this was happening and, as a company, we stepped in to support her as best as we could. What happened next was a big surprise: other Certified Consultants stepped in and handled her clients for her, passing all the revenue back to her. They continued to do this for months while she recovered. The bond and show of good will was energizing and led to bringing the whole group closer.

When you build your culture and your group deliberately, knowing the pitfalls and the potential accelerators, you will have an incredibly supportive network of people who surpass your own employees in regard to loyalty and service.

This is a killer competitive advantage. I have done it wrong and paid the price, and I have done it right and reaped the benefits. I can tell you from experience that it is worth doing it right!

This "Culture Thing" I've been talking about is the secret sauce to success. Ignore this, and you will be sorry you did. If I hadn't personally screwed this up myself and then had to repair it, I would never have realized the importance of this concept. Ignore this at your peril.

WHERE DO YOU GET YOUR CULTURE FROM?

You create it. I work directly with my clients to consciously create their culture, and over the years, I have developed tools to help do this.

We start with the basic values of how we want to treat each other and our clients. We then move to defining what is right and wrong. Is it wrong to take the company's intellectual property and copy it freely, or populate your website with the company's "stuff" and not get permission? Or worse, make it look like your own?

This document, the Code of Ethics, is designed to create that safe environment I discussed before. This means anticipating what could happen and what is likely to happen when you have a hundred or several hundred people, all outside the company, as independent vendors to the company.

Deliberately build your culture code and practice it. Create a course all new applicants must take, and ask them to sign a document that proves they understand what your culture is, and how they must act. If Certified Consultants graduate from your program and adhere to the culture, they will feel safe and enabled, and they will be supported throughout the process. This is what we want, and we will take responsibility for making it so.

A Culture Code can be short or long; it can be stated in business terms or in the spirit of a family. Every new client I work with gets the "starter" kit, which is my own broad stroke culture statements I've used for many years.

Some of the issues you need to cover in your own culture document and training:

» Who owns the intellectual property?

» What can be shared independently, and what is considered confidential?

» To what extent can a Certified Consultant represent themselves with your brand? Can they do interviews? Webinars? Advertise on Facebook?

» How does a Certified Consultant present themselves?

» How do they treat each other?

» What are the rules about competition?

» What if they have staff? Do they, too, have to be certified?

» What responsibilities does a Certified Consultant have to their (your) client?

» Can a Certified Consultant work with a client outside the company relationship?

» What happens if these "rules" are broken?

» Is there a "guarantee" on the work that Certified Consultants perform?

» Who resolves the issues created?

This is a small sample of the issues you need to address up front, before you even train your first student. Doing so will change their perspective in a powerful way. This type of document provides boundaries, and those are welcome and needed in any thriving community or society. It also makes it clear what happens if there are problems and how they are handled.

As a successful business person, you know that boundaries are welcome in a healthy environment; they allow for freedom of expression and create archetypes that our Certified Consultants can aspire to. They also visibly indicate when someone is not performing within the cultural norms and needs to be called out.

For example, is it okay for a new Certified Consultant to take your content and publish it on his or her own website? If not, make this clear up front. Also, with a supportive, enriching culture, others in the community will spot that and tell the offender to fix it before you ever find out. That's what I mean by self-correcting.

There are so many other ways culture plays a role in the success of well-run programs that they become hard to name. When you start with your "Why" and build your culture from there, then much of what you say is an extension of what you've already shown yourself to represent. Even when specific deeds are not covered in the code, the spirit of your culture will point people in the right direction.

The best culture is one that is practically invisible - yet allows for full self-expression and advancement. Use that as your guide when you build yours and it will be hard to make a mistake.

One other point I want to make: Once you complete your culture code, create a course in your Learning Management System that covers it and tests for comprehension. This way, there's never an excuse when the inevitable mistake is made. If everyone must pass the quiz with a 100% grade, then you know they have received the message loud and clear. You are simply saying to your group that boundaries exist for your own protection and the protection of the Tribe itself.

CHAPTER EIGHT

HOW DO YOU CREATE A MOVEMENT

HOW TO CREATE A MOVEMENT

THIS CHART COMES FROM A presentation given by Russell Brunson. He built a powerful software product called "ClickFunnels," which became almost an instant success. He talks about "creators" as those of us who are creating "works of art" (our products) and claims that all you need is 1,000 true fans to build a company. Note: ClickFunnels is a registered trademark.

As our fans go through the process of starting as a student and eventually becoming a teacher, they become even better as both a user of our processes and systems and as a guide. As I am sure you have observed, unless you contribute to the lives of others, you cannot grow beyond what you can learn on your own.

You grow through teaching others, sharing your wisdom and processes so that others can benefit greatly by the work you pioneered.

Your Certification students will think about how this might be scary, which is normal. Acknowledge their fear and commend them on their courage; assure them that they are on the right track. They will lose the fear as they gain experience and see the results of their actions. Watch as they develop a deep confidence and find their true voice.

THE CHARISMATIC CHARACTER; THE ATTRACTIVE CHARACTER

Live the life your audience seeks to live. Lead by example; show people what you have done, so they will bond with you and be attracted to wanting a life like you've designed for yourself. On one level, help them aspire to be like you. This will motivate them to take that step; to step into the life you want them to have. If they are going to "become" you, the goal is to make that as attractive as possible to those who know you. You may not think you are exciting and charismatic, but if you are passionate about your mission and your goals, then you can display that passion when you communicate through video and writing to your tribe.

YOUR CERTAINTY AND YOUR CONFIDENCE

If you are going to be a leader, maintain absolute certainty, even if you are not entirely there yet. "Act as if..." is a common catchphrase, but it's rooted in the truth of human nature. When you do, you become more like what you think you are pretending to be.

Be completely certain in who you are and what you do, and people will be attracted to you when they see that you know what is working and can demonstrate success. This starts by lightening up and showing you are enjoying your life and having fun.

WHAT IT TAKES TO BE A LEADER OF YOUR TRIBE.

Be highly communicative, be and act special in an inviting way. Being normal is not so attractive, but making a bold claim, stepping out of your comfort zone, and being consistently provocative yet upbeat and positive certainly is. Being a leader means you can lead by being you *out loud*. Not in secret and not quietly. Be You. Be Loud. Have Fun!

STARTING OUT AS A MARKET LEADER.

No one I know enters a market that's already heavily populated with vendors and declares they are the leader unless you are Apple and releasing an iPod. For our work, it's all about creating a market, not picking one. This is commonly referred to as a "Blue Ocean Strategy" from the popular business book: Blue Ocean Strategy - How to Create Uncontested Market Space and Make the Competition Irrelevant by W Chan Kim.

When you pick a market, you are already competing with those in it. Before you know it, that market is crowded, and you are one of many. But when you create a market, you are the leader of that market, and you are building a competitive barrier with your own market. By building your own Tribe around your own products, you are creating your market; but if you don't capitalize on it, others will nudge you out and do it for you. If you are building your PowerTribe Certification Program, then you are most definitely creating a new market of which you are now the declared leader. Here's a good example of how that works.

MARKETS AND SUB-MARKETS, AND WHY YOU CARE

Think about Infusionsoft. They have an automated marketing system. A lot of people have automated marketing systems, but Infusionsoft created their own market that was new: the Infusionsoft market. Inside that market is the ecosystem which they created. There are Certified Consultants, tool vendors, trainers, services – all part of a market that didn't exist until Infusionsoft created it. That's what I want you to do! Create your market around you and your products, and you will own the whole ecosystem. Forever.

CREATING THE CAUSE

All great movements have a future-based cause. You are building a great movement, and it will attract people who want to put their hope and faith into you.

Show them a "new world" where they can use what you teach them to recreate themselves into a better version of themselves. Sell a new future that is appealing, attractive, and hold the promise of a better life. In a real sense, you are offering a person a change from what they have into something different: a bright future as a Certified Consultant.

It's best to sell a future-based cause. That's what builds dreams in others. When someone dreams of a new life, that motivator is stronger than simply looking at a business opportunity. If you are attracted to the lifestyle of the leader – the cause (the "Why") of the leader – then you are showing them more than just a way to make money, you are offering them a new life.

This new life is "living the dream". When we build a PowerTribe, we are creating a group of people who are moving closer and closer to living the dream.

Some will get "there" quickly, while others will need your help. Those who do will, with your guidance, end up being your greatest and most loyal fans, usually for life.

RECOGNITION OF THE RESULTS OF LIVING THE DREAM

When we build our PowerTribe Certification system, we start with the business model as Phase One of our build-out. Then, we move into implementing all the plans we created in Phase One: the learning management system, the culture, the selling opportunities, the back-end management system, and the launch.

After our first-class graduates, we will do we can to make these people as successful as possible. This is how we show others what's possible by joining the movement and becoming part of your PowerTribe. That's how we create the dream over and over again: by showing them success in others.

Those people who become successful are living the dream and must be recognized for having accomplished the end result. This obviously becomes your most powerful selling tool for new recruits AND the goal for every new person who joins your program. Give them their social media badge, Certificate, and t-shirt. Give them a briefcase with your logo emblazoned on it, with the words Certified Consultant under it. This is status.

Show them that others who came before them, others just like them, have accomplished great things. If Mary can do it, then so can you, and here's how she did it and what she accomplished. There's nothing more empowering than a great testimonial coming from a person who started at the beginning. That recognition is gold.

HELP THEM BOND THROUGH IDENTITY

The simple idea is to make your Tribe's mission hold a higher level of status.

» What is your manifesto?

» What can people rally around?

» What do we stand for?

» What do we NOT stand for?

» Who DOESN'T belong?

These questions are the fabric of your thinking and philosophy, even if you don't think you have one. Each of the above questions can be components of your culture, your code of ethics.

WHAT IS THE NEW OPPORTUNITY? WHAT IS THE VEHICLE OF CHANGE?

Most people are selling an improvement (better, smarter, faster), but the problem is that they first have to admit that they are not already good, smart, or fast.

We don't want to help people to become better; we want to offer a new opportunity.

This is what we emphasize in our launch. Building the launch (covered in a later chapter) starts by explaining what's wrong with the world. As your video series progresses, you show that you acknowledge that an era is coming to an end and a new era is beginning. You are the savior; the one to herald in the new year using your Certification Program.

Improvement is hard. This is not the first time people have tried to improve, and there is a lot of pain tied to past attempts at improvement. Selling improvement means you need to find ambitious people who have failed many times trying to improve. Improvement is a commodity, but a new opportunity is not a place where most people have failed before; there's no pain there. All they need is the desire to take advantage of a new life.

Every buying decision your potential clients make is based on status. Is this decision going to increase my status or decrease my status? Decreasing status is all about what you don't want to stand for versus how you can show the world that are special and different in a really good way. This is why most people buy or don't buy.

New opportunities are new discoveries that can increase your status by showing you are sharing something new. This raises your status as a person who discovers new opportunities. With an improvement offer, there's the pain of disconnect and failure; but with a new opportunity, there is no pain of disconnect.

HOW DO YOU PRESENT AND CREATE A NEW OPPORTUNITY?

Potentially, there are three types of people who will consider purchasing Certification from your company:

1. The first is the know-it-all: the person who wants to be sure he knows everything 100%. It may be because he works for a company and he's the local resident expert, or maybe it's just the way his personality works.

2. The person looking for change. They took advantage of an opportunity, but it's not working out as well as it has previously, and they are looking to move on. It may also be that they never really tried anything new but are willing to do so now.

3. The opportunity "stack." These folks want to add a new opportunity to the existing opportunity they already have in place. They are already working toward the dream, and they want to get there faster by stacking opportunities.

PRESENTING A NEW OPPORTUNITY!

The opportunity you are suggesting is to leave something behind and switch into something new, with a higher promise and level of success.

Certification is a full-blown program your company is offering. Your company is committed to creating a powerful, meaningful program. Once they are Certified, then you can offer even more opportunities within the new opportunity you sold to them. They can start with Certification Level One, then move to Level Two, followed by Mentorship, Mastery, Mastermind, and finally into the Inner Circle and whatever else you create in the future to deepen and enhance the ONE opportunity in which you now have them involved.

This program is a revolution for your industry, where you are the leader. It's not an off-the-shelf product; it's your company enabling others. As the CEO, the idea of risk comes up in my discussions.

Are we risking our core market by enabling others to do what we do?

Generally, not, because you control the business model, the training systems, and the back end. If you do this right, you will also control the flow of prospects and customers. When carefully designed, your PowerTribe Certification Program will become a revolution in your industry because not many companies go to the extent you will when you build your Program. Remember: as successful as Infusionsoft and Intuit are, they don't have all the multiple streams of recurring revenue or the strong culture you are creating now.

Welcome to <u>your</u> revolution. Your Tribe is waiting for you!

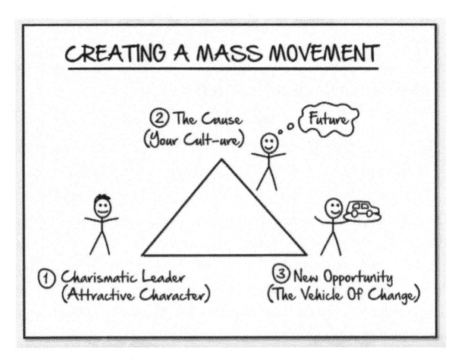

CHAPTER NINE

The 12 Commandments

———————

THE BIBLICAL STORY OF MOSES and the 10 Commandments works well as an analogy for what we are doing. If you remember, Moses came down from Mt. Sinai and saw his followers in chaos, worshiping idols and conducting themselves in inappropriate ways. Without the guidance of the 12 Commandments of Building a Power Tribe, you might find yourself in the same position as Moses when you see the chaos that ensues from an unstructured plan with no boundaries.

That's why I am summarizing some of the most important lessons here, sans the solid rock tablets. These are the specific values which have emerged from my work, which I can share with you so you won't need to struggle with this as so many have.

THE 12 COMMANDMENTS OF BUILDING A POWERTRIBE CERTIFICATION PROGRAM

Here are the values I depend on when building this type of organization for clients:

1. Your PowerTribe must become fully integrated into the structure of your company. This means that your PowerTribe must be valued with the same (or greater) weight as your own staff, even (sometimes) over the sales force.

2. All marketing must first consider the impact it will have on your PowerTribe and be modified or created to enhance their relationship with the company and their income.

3. Before certifying a single individual to join your PowerTribe, you must train them to 100% competency, not 97%, and not leave them on their own to figure it out.

4. You must establish and communicate the ethical values of your company, its culture, and its creed, along with the founder's "Why," before anyone is admitted into your program.

5. Certified Consultants must abide by that code of ethics to remain part of the Tribe. NOTE: For my private clients, I have created a 38-point "Code of Ethics," which is my core document I use to cover that requirement.

6. I suggest doing a thorough background check on ANYONE you allow into your PowerTribe, so that you don't end up with a deadbeat, sex offender, or neo-Nazi on your team. (Don't laugh, it's happened.)

7. I suggest having a proper contract that spells out exactly how people will qualify, and how often they renew their Certification to remain in the program. This contract must spell out every aspect of who pays who, and when and what restrictions your Certification carries.

8. I highly recommend having an air-tight non-disclosure agreement so ownership of your intellectual property can never be vague, including making sure you state exactly where and how your IP can be used by your PowerTribe members. This can be integrated into your vendor agreement that every Certified Consultant must sign before they are admitted into the training system.

9. It would be best for all your CCs/Consultants to work with you as a vendor to your company, not as an independent contractor, so you stay out of trouble with the local taxing authorities. The result of not doing this will land you in court fighting the state, which is all about trying to bill you for back taxes on all your "independent contractors," who <u>they</u> will have reclassified as employees. You can certainly hire them as employees, but this is very expensive and doesn't yield a team that wants the result as much as they want a paycheck.

10. Be totally upfront (tell the 100% truth) about the current state of the company, the intention of management when it comes to building this type of Tribe, and who they report to inside your organization for each area of their need.

11. To take this one step further, be completely open and honest about everything, so no "dirt" remains to be found. This could seriously undermine your trusted relationship and destroy your program within hours.

12. The company CEO/Owner must be willing to reach out to CCs and engage them directly. Without this direct outreach, the deep connection will be harder to make. Furthermore, the CEO should encourage employees to work with CCs to ensure their success.

With these values, you can begin the planning the building of a network that should be sustainable for many years to come.

One more note about values: be intentional about building this program. These are the human beings who will evolve with you and your company. Encourage your staff to get involved and share with them exactly what you are doing and why you are building this program.

If you aren't sure you want the responsibility (or the incredible benefit) of having your own PowerTribe, get "sure" or don't start building one –

it will fall apart if you are not dedicated to actively maintaining it and fostering its growth.

THE 13th COMMANDMENT

Negativity will destroy your PowerTribe from the inside out. This means that if anyone on your team is negative or skeptical beyond reasonable due diligence, then you must remove them from the process, preferably from the company. This insidious force will destroy your good work one person at a time and sink your chances of success.

The same holds true for newly--recruited Certified Consultants. It's already part of your Code of Ethics, but be on the lookout for that person inside the tribe who is always complaining, always critical, and always looking for what's wrong, not for what's right.

If you've been in business for any length of time, you've probably experienced this type of person and know the destruction they can cause. In one company, I had to fire the entire customer service team because one person had so infected the environment that it was impossible to recover. Six weeks later, we had a whole new team, and everyone loved their job and the company. Sales through customer services began to break records.

Ignore this at your own peril; it's more important than you may believe.

You can download an infographic of the 13 Commandments at: PowerTribesBook.com/13-Commandments

CHAPTER TEN

PRICING AND LAUNCHING YOUR CERTIFICATION PROGRAM

PRICING AND BUILDING YOUR LAUNCH FOR YOUR CERTIFICATION PROGRAM

SETTING THE PRICE IS CRITICAL to the success of your program. It's better to make it more expensive and offer deeper discounts than making it inexpensive up front. It's easier to go down in price than the other way around. As I mentioned earlier, I have clients who priced their program as low as $5,000 and as high as $30,000. The most important element of your pricing is your proof of Return on Investment (ROI), which you will build a case for as you sell.

Traditionally, coaches and consultants who have built a successful business spent years perfecting their intellectual property, their "enrollment conversation" (the sales pitch), and then the justification for the fees they charge. We have to do the same as well as come up with the reasons why someone would want to enroll in your program NOW.

Some of the most significant justifications, voiced as if you were speaking to the group as a whole, are:

1. You get to leverage our reputation and authority when you present yourselves to clients as a Certified Consultant.

2. We have spent years developing our systems for delivery of our transformational process, and you don't have to.

3. We know exactly what outcomes to expect when you apply our materials exactly as we say.

4. We know there is a demand for the services you will deliver.

5. We have internal systems we use to ensure the success of our clients, to which you will get access when you join us.

6. We believe that, compared to anything else, our offer is significantly better because no one else does exactly what we do.

7. You will be completely trained and start working in this business in less than 60 days (or whatever number you feel is accurate).

Other justifications for starting now by introducing urgency are:

» This is a "pilot program" and, as such, it will be a little rough around the edges; we ask you to be patient as we iron those out.

» You will get significantly more attention and help in being successful by helping us perfect the program for the next wave of students.

» We need you to be successful because in the future we may want to offer you a mentorship position in our community.

» You will get a huge discount, up to 25%, for enrolling now instead of waiting for the next wave, and we are not sure when that next wave will be.

» During the pilot, you will have access to everyone in the company to help, but later classes will have just a program manager.

The most powerful element of your program should come LAST after you've highlighted all the reasons why joining now is important. Here's your most powerful and persuasive argument:

"Unlike any other Certified Consultant program that we know of, you will get live leads to work with so that you can build your business starting on Day One. No one else is willing to go to this extent because it's hard, it's expensive, and it requires a lot of time and expertise. Even our sales force is only a little jealous but they know we are all one family working together towards a common goal.

"We will spend up to and beyond the cost of your Certification to generate leads for you because we know that if you are successful, you will want to stay with us for many years to come. We are in this for the long game, we play to win, and we know we need you to help us get there."

Offering your program to your existing clients can happen via a live appearance or through email and videos.

LAUNCHING YOUR PROGRAM FROM YOUR STAGE

The launch of your Certification Program is where you offer your existing clients the chance to become certified and, if they graduate, a member in good standing of your ongoing program. In my experience, there are two ways to launch your program. You can launch it from the stage at an event, or you can launch it using a Jeff Walker-style email launch.

If you are launching from the stage, prepare to spend most of the morning or afternoon working up to that moment where you will send everyone running to the back of the room, credit card in hand. That prep work will make a huge difference in how much buy-in you get when you announce.

Launching from the stage has another huge benefit: you've already built a bond with the people in the room. They spent their money to be there with you and your company, so now is the time to capitalize on that moment and share your success by offering this exclusive group your new program. Allow for plenty of questions, the same questions you may receive if they were responding to an offer by email. Bring in guests who have been working with the company as a Consultant or coach and let them share their success stories. Finally, make sure you have your pricing structure all worked out, along with a significant discount for your first "pilot" class.

Then, when the moment is right, create the scarcity by explaining that you can only accept a limited number of people into the pilot program, and those who enroll today will also get more attention and help than future classes will.

Since you are speaking from the stage, tell stories about how you arrived at the decision to create a program like this. Explain how the market is growing so quickly that you don't have the internal staff to service all the business you know is coming soon.

Reinforce your "Why" as the CEO, making it clear you are here to change the world, and that it's your obligation to bring your "transformation" to as many people and companies as possible. Without a program like this, it will take more time, and many people will be deprived of the life-changing effect of what you do. You are inviting people on a journey to change the world with you and make great money while doing it.

Stress the community aspect of this program. Make it clear that when they join, each member is now part of an inner circle they share with others having the same experiences. Make it clear that their support is vital to your future and the future of the company, and possibly even mankind itself!

Think of the concentric circles of life, with the single individual in the middle. The next ring out would be their family, then their neighborhood and city, then the country, and then the world. Explain how joining you in your mission will benefit them at every level. Show in detail the exact effect their work would have on their work would have on their lives and on the world around them. Make this personal, make it holistic, and make it empowering. Yes, the money will come if they build their business using your tools to help them get there.

One important note: I have never seen this done successfully on a webinar or tele-conference. It takes several days of live interaction and bonding before a buying decision can be made. So, if you won't be launching from stage, then launch through video and email.

LAUNCHING YOUR PROGRAM THROUGH EMAIL

Everything I've mentioned above is completely relevant when it comes to building your online launch plan. If you are familiar with Jeff Walker's Product Launch Formula, which is a time-tested and proven method for launching new products and services, you will feel at home with what I am about to explain.

Launching through email requires two assets you don't need when you launch from the stage:

» Your Infusionsoft (or comparable software) funnel.

» Your professionally-written email sequence.

If this is going to work the way you want and fill your pilot class in about a week, then it's worth doing the up-front work to create these assets so that it goes smoothly.

We have our own resources to create all of this, so when I manage the creation of a PowerTribe Certification Program for my clients, I line all of this up as part of our work together. This is critical to a successful launch because it maximizes the impact of the event you've created. The launch is your event; it's worth taking the time to do it right.

The basic steps are as follows:

1. Send an email to tease your audience that something awesome is about to happen and that they should watch their email for an announcement.

2. Send the first video, which usually highlights the changing environment of how things are "different" and what that means to the reader.

3. The next day, send the next video, which focuses on how you plan on solving the problem you presented in your first video.

4. The following day, send the third and final video which reveals the entire program, including of all the benefits to those who are ready.

5. One day later, send an email which explains how the class is almost full, and that if they are serious about working with you, they need to fill out the application right away.

6. Finally, send one last email explaining that the program has closed, but that if anyone wants to be on the waiting list for those that don't make it through the application process, they should immediately fill out the application.

Note: This is an abbreviated version of the Launch Formula introduced by Jeff Walker and universally known throughout the internet marketing community.

That's it. By then, you should have filled your pilot class. Assuming you ran through the three questions I posed at the beginning of the book, which ensure that you have a transformational product, can teach it to others, and have at least 500 clients, then getting twenty to sign up should be achievable.

Congratulations! Your journey is about to begin with your new partners who are anxious to help you find more customers, support your clients, speak on your behalf, and make a great living while they do it.

THE APPLICATION PROCESS

I have found that it's better to require that someone qualify to be part of something important than to reduce it to a sale. After all, we don't want everyone who would apply. We know they may not be suited for the task at hand. They may be beginners; they may be spending their last dollar in the world; they may not be able to dedicate the time to accomplish the end result. That's why we have an application.

PEOPLE WILL APPLY FOR DIFFERENT REASONS:

The application asks basic questions about who is applying, what their experience has been in a related field, and what their current business is all about. Some of the people who are applying are going to add your services to their existing coaching or consulting practice. Some will want the prestige of adding your company's name and reputation to theirs, and some will be looking to level up their skills and find new clients. We need to know who we are admitting into our program so that we can make sure the experiences they have will benefit them as well as the other members of the community.

As I have pointed out several times, we are building a community of people, and the wrong people should not be allowed in. That is part of what we want our application to do: to help us screen out those who don't belong and screen in the ones who do.

The people who don't belong may not be obvious at first pass. For example, here are a few types of applicants we are screening out:

1. This is their last dollar and they are borrowing the money to buy Certification.

2. They do not have a source of income and have not for some time. Someone who is making a career change is not who we are talking about here.

3. They are negative and it's obvious. When asked about their past performance, they blame others for their failure. Stay away from those.

4. They want a "bargain," or want to negotiate the price. They don't understand the value proposition you are offering, and probably won't in the future.

Finally, the application itself should require a small amount of money to ensure that the person who is filling it out is seriously interested in the opportunity we are offering. The $200-$500 application fee should be fully refunded if they don't qualify.

One other technique I advise my clients to use is to place a scheduling link at the end of the application sequence, so that when they do pay for their application submission, we immediately schedule their interview. The interview is critical to gauge how serious the applicant is when it comes to joining our program. In this interview, we want to question some of the information they provided. We want to find out what their real motivation is to become part of our world and get Certified. We want them driven by our vision and by their commitment and desire to make a great living.

Remember, this is your closing call. It we like the candidate and they are a good fit for the program, we enroll them and take a credit card on the spot.

Once, in an application interview, I was informed that the candidate was applying because his company wanted him to; they wanted someone on staff who can work inside with those skills. He wasn't that motivated and didn't seem like he would fit into the community, so we rejected him. Yet it's certainly possible that someone inside another company can be a great member of the community. That's okay if they seem excited to get going and want to be fully committed.

WHEN TO STOP SELLING

You should be able to reach twenty confirmed and paid candidates in about a week. I recommend overbooking by a couple of people because almost immediately three people will drop out and ask for their money back. Between two-thirds and three-quarters of those who pay will pay in full. The rest will pay using a payment plan, and the drop-outs usually come from the payment plan group.

If we have over-recruited by a few, we are fine. Statistically up to 20% can drop out of the pilot class for several reasons: not really having the funds available, not having the time available, not having enough life or business experience to have confidence that they will succeed, or simply because the material is too difficult for them to comprehend.

CLOSING THE PILOT CLASS AT (ABOUT) TWENTY PEOPLE

We do this because we know that the pilot program will not be perfect; it will require some fine-tuning as our new students are making their way through the program. We restrict enrollment to twenty people so that we know we can handle whatever comes up while we're taking those people through our course. If a new person is hired as your Program Manager, they too were getting used to all of the new systems that are in place to support them. That's why we are careful not to go with more than twenty people – so we don't put too much stress on our personnel and on our systems, which are still being perfected.

Now that your program is filled and you understand the process of how this all works, it's time to deliver a fantastic experience to your new business partners and make sure they are excited about your collective future!

CHAPTER ELEVEN

CREATING A PROFESSION FOR YOUR CONSULTANTS

YEARS AGO, WHEN A COACH wanted to become a coach, they went to a coaching organization and purchased "Certification," which for many people was the beginning of a new profession. Those early pioneers of the coaching world learned the lessons I am about to share with you the hard way. Today, you get them free as part of the experience you are having from reading this book; but they were not free when it came to learning these lessons. Not for me, not for the coaching companies who came before me, and not for those companies today who are desperately searching for a way to create new revenue models because the old one has stopped working.

My friend Ken Courtright, the CEO of The Income Store, says in his highly informative podcast that all current sources of revenue will die. His example is those people who started companies 50 years ago, most of which are out of business. They are out because of entropy, nature's way of returning everything living and made from the materials on this planet back to their natural elements. The return to chaos.

Ken suggests that because of the times we live in, this is happening to companies at a faster pace than ever before. Entropy starts with product lines; they launch, they grow, they peak, and then they decay back to zero.

This is natural; as I said above, it's a law of nature. How does this apply to us? Remember, we are offering to create a new profession for our prospective Certified Consultants. This will become their new income/revenue cycle. If we do our jobs correctly, if we stay focused on great products and fantastic service, we will be here long enough for our Certified Consultants to grow and mature their little practice into a mid-six-figure business. After all, that's the goal of any good business opportunity.

Yes, we are offering a business opportunity, but a far more comprehensive one than those that come from fly-by-night franchise companies or multi-level marketing companies. We are offering a PROFESSION. We can say this because our Certification clients are becoming trained professionals with the systems we are putting in place to train them, grow their skills, create leads and opportunities, and even ascend through the ranks of our own program. Now that's value.

It fits into the bigger picture of what's happening in the world today as we speak to almost every industry and profession, and it's the story you can relay to those considering joining your ranks to be in your PowerTribe.

Fifty years ago, there were companies who had a work force. Many who went to work expected to retire after 30 years, and then slow down. Then things changed, and we needed two incomes to run a nice middle-class household with a few kids who like eating and wearing clothing. And don't forget saving for college that kept increasing in price faster than the average income could keep up.

About 30 years ago, it became the age of the Independent Contractor. These folks quit their jobs and were rehired at double or triple their pay to work at the same company, but without benefits or vacation time. That went well for a while, until Uncle Sam realized that those same companies weren't paying employee taxes and the government was losing revenue. So they cracked down on many of the companies who employed those Independent Contractors, and made them pay.

Things changed again when it became clear that a lot of those high-paying posts were disappearing under the pressure from the taxing authorities, several recessions, and a change in attitude among company leadership.

Next came the educated, skilled, independent company, operating as a corporation of one. The tax man liked her; she was paying both her employee and employer taxes, and now she sold results instead of hourly services. It was a quiet revolution that started when a guy named Tony Robbins offered coaching at the professional level for the first time.

Now, things are again different. Now we have the "consultant," who knows they have a very specialized skill that can command a high fee but that they also must quickly deliver a powerful result. These people are the foot soldiers of business today, and they are infiltrating our businesses and government to inject skill and wisdom exactly where it's needed and when it's needed before moving on to the next candidate.

The specialization is at its peak, and the results must be proven by powerful testimonials or by the guarantee of the sponsoring company. This is our goal: to create an army of powerful, highly-trained experts who know how to cause a massive transformation – your transformation – quickly and effectively in exchange for a large sum of money.

This is the story behind why Certified Consultants are in their prime of life, why you are a pivotal element in their professional trajectory, and why they will demand from you the utmost quality of training and service.

Another way to look at this is that you are creating an army of angels, each capable of a special blessing – the one you taught them to deliver. When delivered, their clients are endowed with new powers and skills, which funnel directly from you.

Now we can see what the appeal is to those who want to be Certified Consultants; they want to create miracles in the lives of others (and this includes transformations in companies) while getting paid great money for their magic. For your magic, which actually flows through them.

When you tell this story in your launch videos and share the new world with your prospective Certified Consultants, it should resonate with those who already know what you do, have experienced your transformation, who know the value of it when applied to the right person or company.

This is what you sell: you are selling a rare opportunity to learn and perform your magic. And why not help them create the miracles you perform if you get to keep 50% of their income for setting them up with your leads?

And they will welcome the opportunity to be of service. It's their calling, as well, and armed with your weapons of mass transformation, they will have an explosive effect on the world that surrounds them. Usually that world would not be affected by you directly since it's their locality. It will be their good reputation and community standing that is the first pillar of trust they rest on when introducing their new super power. They are also supported by your pillar, knowing that your company backs them and has their interests at heart.

What could be better than that? It's the whole enchilada all wrapped up and ready to serve and satisfy a hungry audience that doesn't even know what Mexican food tastes like. But one client later and they are hooked; using all your tech and your magic, your Certified Consultant has a new client of their own while sharing the bounty at each stage of the game with you.

Everyone wins.

CHAPTER TWELVE

HOW INFUSIONSOFT, MICROSOFT, AND INTUIT BUILT THEIR PROGRAMS

S OME OF THE BIGGEST COMPANIES in the world use Certification as a way to generate sales and service revenue every day. The companies you probably associate with regularly have Certified Consultants, and you may have even hired one to assist you in implementing one of those products. I want to show you some examples of programs that large companies create. If you understand the level of impact their Certification Programs have in their business, you will be even more motivated to start working on your own.

Let's take a look at Infusionsoft.

If you don't know who they are, go to Infusionsoft.com, and you will see that they host a cloud-based application that allows their clients to manage customer relationships from prospects through the sales process. In fact, most of my clients use Infusionsoft to launch their own Certification Programs.

If you were to become a Certified Consultant in the Infusionsoft Certified Partner Program, the major benefits are:

1. Reseller privileges, which allows you make a commission on every client you start using the Certification system;

2. Monthly recurring revenue ranging from 20% to 30% for having signed that client and keeping them committed to the product;

3. Inclusion in the private online forum to network with other Infusionsoft partners;

4. The "credentials" that allow you to say that you are Infusionsoft Certified;

5. A higher level of tech support than the average customer gets;

6. Specific training just for Certified Partners;

7. Access to the codebase through API (links into the software) so that you can build an add-on and sell it;

8. Invitation to their premier event called PartnerCon, which generates a great deal of revenue for the company in many ways. Those Value-Added-Resellers (VARs,) which are generating more revenue for the company, get better rates when they pay for their attendance every year.

Besides learning how to use the system, you have access to their marketing and training programs, so you become an extension of their sales force, which is what we spoke about earlier. They have a culture program which hits the highlights of how a Certified Partner should behave, including the expectations, guidelines, and policies they must adhere to.

Another very smart thing that Infusionsoft does is to offer a tiered service offering. There are VARs, Service Partners, and App Developers. All are charged a fee for participation, and each level has a different experience level requirement.

"PAY ONCE" POLICY WITH INFUSIONSOFT.

Infusionsoft has a "pay once" policy for their Certified Consultants. The reason for this is that they focus heavily on converting many of those people into a very active sales force. The exception to that rule is their Service Partner level, which pays just $2,000 to enter the program and $1,500 a year to renew.

There are several intricate levels and layers of participation based on a metric they call "Customer Health," which may determine your continued future as a Service Provider or Certified Consultant. To see the entire program, go here: https://files.Infusionsoft.com/partners.Infusionsoft.com/program_guide_final_version.pdf

MICROSOFT IS A HYBRID MODEL

Microsoft is one of those companies who sells their training levels with Certification. Using that credential, those who take part in their training programs and pay a higher price get the credential. In the tech world, having a Microsoft Certification means you know how to use the technology. Microsoft does not train people on how to sell their products, and on the surface, I can't find anything about discounts and commissions; but Microsoft's Certification System has educated many technical people, which benefits the company both competitively and financially.

While Microsoft's Certification Training is nothing like the Certification Systems covered in this book, their system serves as proof of how valuable their Certified Partners can be to the company at every level in the sales and delivery cycle.

INTUIT AND THEIR CERTIFIED PROADVISOR PROGRAM

Possibly the most valuable example of an integrated Certification Program that is most like the programs I build is the one that Intuit has been running for years. As I mentioned earlier, the former CEO and founder of Intuit, Scott Cook, modeled the original ProAdvisor Program after my own Timeslips Certified Consultant Program back in 1989. I won't repeat the story, but their current program is still very similar to my original model aside from being updated with the current 2017 technology and systems.

Intuit offers two types of certification: QuickBooks Online Certification and QuickBooks Online Advanced Certification. The Advanced Certification goes deeper into the technology, training the Advanced Advisors to perform a complex conversion and apply in-depth customizations to QuickBooks Online in a way that the standard ProAdvisor does not know how to do.

You can ascend in their program by certifying at higher levels and paying more fees or by generating more new client signups. Certification gets accountants entry into a universal directory which is accessed by 600,000 small businesses. You have additional access to more courses, and you get discounts on products for reseller status. You can also buy ads in their directory, which is another significant revenue driver for the program and the company.

Other benefits include custom applications and services only available to the Certified ProAdvisor that differentiate him or her from the average CPA. Intuit has done such an incredible job of becoming the "standard" accounting solution for small business primarily because of their ProAdvisor program. By enrolling thousands of accountants and giving them the training and guidelines to accept client data files in QuickBook format, they own the client for life. This benefits the accountant, the client, and the company in a very significant way.

More recently, Quickbooks has migrated entirely online and now certified Intuit Accountants can host their clients under their login and manage multiple individual companies from one access point. And, when a client buys online access, the Quickbooks Certified Accountant gets a small share of the monthly fee.

Just remember, the Intuit QuickBooks Certified ProAdvisor Program started with just a few dozen CPAs who were interested in learning more about QuickBooks. As you begin your program, keep in mind that you, too, are at the beginning of a potentially gigantic evolution of your company and your marketplace. In one short year or less, you can have your own Certified Consultants in every state and multiple countries selling your products and services. The value cannot be understated, for a well-run program will pay dividends forever.

Who else offers Certification Programs?

» LeadPages.com

» Salesforce.com

» Infusionsoft

» Hubspot Certified Consultant/Partner

» CloudU – Rackspace

» Sage.com – Accounting Product Certification (many)

» IBM Certified Cloud Solution Architect

» Google Certified Deployment Specialist

» VMware Certified Professional

» Red Hat Infrastructure Certification

» AWS Certification

In all of the above programs, the common benefit is having a highly-educated team of people external to the company who are deployable on behalf of the company to solve problems for customers, keep them current with their subscriptions, and help them use advanced features.

Therefore, those who participate generally pay a lot of money to get Certified, stay Certified, and travel to events hosted by the company.

Each company above has a different set of features, benefits, and costs associated with being in their program.

As mentioned earlier in the book, 15% of those who complete any Certification are not looking to earn money as a result of their Certification. Instead, they want to be the best at what they do and are willing to take the time, spend the money, and show up to play and accomplish their goal, which may also be a role in their corporate environment. We love those people in our programs because they support the rest of the group and are happy, feeling that they are important enough to do so. That's why we are careful to make sure they are always included in every program I build.

In the programs I build, we have a re-Certification fee built into the program so that we generate recurring revenue from our Certified Consultants every year. Our goal is to provide a strong ROI – between 3x and 10x their investment every year – so renewing their Certification is never in question. There are always a few outliers who generate as much as 15x or more. Our responsibility is to create an environment along with the support our Certified Consultants need to build their business. We will cover more on that topic in the Marketing Chapter.

THE KEY TAKEAWAYS YOU CAN USE WHEN BUILDING YOUR OWN PROGRAM:

1. Don't overcomplicate your program. The weight of simply under-standing Infusionsoft's program may be overwhelming to some.

2. Go beyond a Certificate. In Microsoft's case, a Certificate is all they ever wanted, which serves their purpose. But it won't serve ours.

3. Add members slowly. Start small and build only as you can fully support your current membership, with horsepower and capacity to spare.

4. Make sure you know your outcome. Do you want to build a con-sultative sales force who generate their living (or a portion of it) on

your services and products? Or are you certifying techs who end up with a Certificate they can use when applying for jobs?

5. Always, always focus on the end user, your ultimate client, making sure they are best served with whatever program you build.

6. What is it that you ultimately want? Do you want to change the world with your program and products, or do you want to generate a bankroll of cash? You can do both, but if you take the higher ground, your program will serve a higher purpose and eventually create the cash flow you want.

CONCLUSION.

Stay focused on your outcome and remember that your Pilot Program is designed to be a minimally viable product that you will perfect and refine over many years to come.

CHAPTER THIRTEEN

NEXT STEPS: THE RECURRING REVENUE

HOW YOUR PROGRAM WILL GENERATE MULTIPLE STREAMS OF RECURRING REVENUE

WHENEVER I OFFER MY PROGRAM to a potential client, I make the claim that we will create at least four new recurring revenue streams for their business that they never had before. At first, it seems almost too good to be true; but after I'm done explaining it, my clients see exactly how that happens. Here are some of the ways to create recurring revenue in your organization using Certification:

Yearly Certification fees are just one source of recurring revenue. If you sign a new Certified Consultant, they will pay you $6,000 to $30,000 to become Certified.

Next year, you can require upwards of 50% to stay Certified in your program. The only reason someone would pay you year after year is if they are getting a return on investment from the money they have already spent. It's your job to make sure that they're getting that return on their investment, because when they do, it benefits everybody – the Certified Consultant, the company, and your clients.

At the end of the first year, you should have between 50 and 100 Certified Consultants in your ranks. I highly recommend inviting them every year to a live symposium where you will spend three days showing them plenty of new and wonderful products and services that they will have access to in the following year.

The symposium should be a paid event, where you can charge between $1,000 and $3,000 per person to attend. One simple way to generate more revenue from your symposium is to offer optional training days. If you had an advanced sales training where they would pay an extra $500 and stay over an extra day, many would take you up on that offer. Obviously, that helps you and your company as much as it helps your Certified Consultant. Another way that you could gain additional revenue at your symposium is to offer ascension.

When you started your program, everybody came in at the same level. Let's call those folks protégés. As protégés, they'll earn their way to becoming a full-fledged Certified Consultant by successfully completing several client engagements. During the time they are earning their stripes, they depend on the company for a lot of support. I recommend bringing in a program manager early in the process, so that they become familiar with everything that is happening in the program.

The program manager is responsible for taking care of everybody who is a Certified Consultant. If they don't know how to handle a certain technical aspect of the Certified Consultant's job, it's the program manager's responsibility to find someone who can help them. By the time we have reached the one-year mark, that program manager is pretty busy. You may have already hired a second person to help with the extra work of additional Certified Consultants coming on board.

What would happen if we were to ascend a small group of our original Certified Consultants from protégés to mentors? Let's think about the advantages of this. Mentors will lessen the load of the program manager who is supporting your new Certified Consultants. This will greatly improve the protégé experience because they are mentored by Certified Consultants who've already been working in the field for a year and are now experienced enough to handle almost any client interaction your new Certified Consultant will encounter.

An excellent way to do this is to allow the mentor to share the revenue generated by new Certified Consultants in client engagements. A typical example would be to allow a mentor to take on ten protégés, with each protégé contributing 15% of their client fees. After a certain number of successful client engagements, that protégé no longer needs a mentor.

In fact, next year they may qualify to become a mentor themselves. We can assign a hefty fee to Certified Consultants who want to become mentors. Depending on the number of clients and other aspects of the client engagement cycle, a mentor can generate substantial revenue working with ten protégés. We can charge upwards of $25,000 to $50,000 a year for a mentorship.

Depending on the size of your Certified Consultant organization, you should be able to bring on mentors at the ratio of 20 to 1. If you have 100 people, then offering 5 mentorship spots should be enough. Another element to consider is your program growth rate. Remember, mentors are working with new graduates – protégé's and apprentices who have completed their training but not yet worked with a client. As your Certified Consultant base grows, then more mentors can be assigned.

Mentors can still take on clients themselves, and because of their senior status, they can be relied on to help the company and represent the company in ways that the newer Certified Consultant isn't capable of quite yet.

Having mentors is like having a staff of senior Certified Consultants available to you anytime you need. Mentors can also represent the group. You can call a separate mentor meeting and run new ideas by them first to get their input, so that when you introduce it to you Certified Consultants, you have their backing. It's consensus building at its finest!

Consider your company two years from now having launched your Certification Program. You have several hundred Certified Consultants in the field, you have ten senior mentors out there helping to manage the group, and you are generating several million dollars a year directly from this channel.

Now compare this to the traditional way of building a sales force: spending hundreds of thousands of dollars in salary and commissions, employing many new people with all the overhead involved, and not even knowing how good they will be at their job. Certification weeds out the weak and rewards the strong. Another way of saying this is that those who choose to become Certified are enthusiastically inclined to help your company grow, and they have a great incentive to do so!

IN SUMMARY: YOUR RECURRING REVENUE STREAMS SO FAR ARE:

1. Certification fees for new PowerTribe members.
2. Re-Certification fees next year, typically at 50%-75% of the original fee.
3. Symposium fees along with all the up-sells we discussed.
4. Mentorship Certification Program for experienced CCs.

CHAPTER FOURTEEN

WORKING WITH YOUR TEAM TO GET STARTED

E ARLY ON, I HAD A CLIENT who created a very powerful and popular training program. His launches were flawless, perfectly executed selling machines with professional videos and scripts. All his email messages were written by professional copywriters specializing in launch sequences. As expected, his launch generated several million dollars in a very short period of time.

He came to me realizing that a Certification Program would greatly increase buy-in and follow-through by his clients, establishing his network of offices in every state and several countries. He also completely understood the financial benefits of doing this.

When we started working together, he had a very clear idea about what he wanted his program to accomplish, and we worked together to make sure he would get that specific outcome.

At the end of my "Phase One," we had our plan, our structure, our pricing, and even our launch sequence planed with dates to follow. We were about to enter Phase Two when I spotted a problem.

Usually I look for an existing employee or the founder herself to create the courses I require in our Learning Management System. I have a very specific way I want to see the coursework done because if the work is done in the exact way I specify, students will likely graduate with as close to 100% comprehension of their materials as possible.

Yes, I can be a bit "retentive" about this because of my past experiences. I was part of the team that created Tony Robbins's virtual training environment, which helped me understand what Tony requires. He is the ultimate master coach and trainer, so I took advantage of the chance to learn even more from Tony than I already had.

My client selected a person who was building a group facilitation program to teach his materials inside corporations. I thought that this person would be perfect in the role of course creator.

After we were introduced, I spent over an hour explaining the philosophy of how Certification Training must be done. I felt confident that she fully understood my instructions and was looking forward to starting.

In a personal conversation with the owner of the company, I discovered that she was not being paid. In fact, she wanted to work with the company so badly that she had volunteered to work for free. I immediately sensed that this could be a problem, and I advised my client to come up with a formal contract spelling out exactly what was expected on both sides. I also suggested that this very talented person get compensated for her work.

Unfortunately for the company, they never followed through or built their program. The person who would have been responsible had not "bought in" to the process; she thought she could already do what I was training her to do, and on top of everything else, she resented my presence.

Why would I talk about my unsuccessful assignments instead of only my successful ones? Because there are valuable lessons to be learned from the mistakes we all make. I want you to make sure you don't make those same mistakes.

Here's what should have happened but didn't:

The person I was training to build the Certification Program was not bought in, meaning she didn't want to do it my way. When I am hired to work as a consultant in this regard, my fees are for my advice, guidance, and skills. I also bring my Rolodex to the table, which I use to my clients' advantage. Unfortunately, they received almost none of those benefits.

Since there was no incentive, I received no cooperation, and the company owner never (to this day) built their Certification Program. Not only did millions of dollars get left on the table, but also hundreds of smart people who could have had a new profession as a Certified Consultant for this company's program will never get the chance.

Here's the lesson I learned:

Don't assume that everyone on your team has an incentive to build this program.

Why do they need an incentive? Because it's hard. There is a lot of work, and it takes precise planning and execution to pull it off without a hitch.

If someone is not getting paid to do the work, why would they want to do it? It seems obvious to me now; get your team on board and make sure there's a personal benefit to getting their full attention and cooperation.

KEY QUESTIONS:

» How will they benefit by being involved?

» What can you do to get full buy-in from your internal constituents?

> » Is there a promotion?

> » A pay increase?

> » A royalty or commission on the sale of Certification enrollment fees?

These are all reasonable expectations by anyone who is willing to roll up their sleeves for several months of hard work, on top of the existing work load they are already carrying. Be smart, be generous, and share in the experience and the rewards; it will pay you huge dividends in the end.

Any owner of a company who decides to start building their own Certification Program must be fully committed to supporting their network, knowing that it can take several years to fully develop. In the end, it's worth all of the time and money invested because once it's built, it lasts forever – as long as you treat your Certified Coaches or Consultants like gold.

As I've mentioned earlier, we must embed our training processes and instruction into a software system that will help train our students; our LMS. This training must be followed to the letter and must be highly effective, or our network will falter. Such is the value of building your training program with precision and attention to detail.

Before we go much further, understand that we are all human and make mistakes. Let's use that human quality to our advantage and embrace the process to improve our program.

Remember when I talked about how only 2-5% of your clients will want to buy your Certification Program?

With about 500 clients, we should easily fill our "pilot" class. But the purpose of the pilot class is two-fold:

1. To test all our systems and make sure everything we are doing is working. This beta test is so critical that we plan in advance for

problems and devise ways to track and then correct them. With just 20 people max, the job is manageable; but if you open the program to everyone, your support staff will not be able to handle the onslaught of problems all new programs bring.

2. We need those first Certified Consultants to provide amazing testimonials so that we can help others take the leap and buy into our program.

So what do people who join the Pilot Program get for being Guinea Pigs?

They get a discount on enrollment and they are lavished with attention! This means we over-deliver in a big way to ensure that first "class" is topnotch. If we do, not only will we get great testimonials, we will have a solid base to build the rest of the program on.

Later, I will show you how to create "ascension" in your program so that your most active members can "level up" and become even more involved. Doing so will generate a substantial cash infusion AND begin to relieve the company of its growing support burden. But that comes later in the book.

CHAPTER FIFTEEN

STREAMLINING YOUR BUILDOUT BY USING CONSULTANTS

WORKING WITH A POWERTRIBE EXPERT TO CREATE YOUR CERTIFICATION PROGRAM

B Y NOW, YOU MAY BE CONSIDERING the possibilities of building your own PowerTribe, and I hope this book has provided you with enough information to get started. You may have read this far and thought that it was too complex or time-consuming. It is NOT complex, but it is time-consuming. There are many steps to take, and there are several areas where small errors can have a huge negative effect.

Our company does all the organization and planning for a fully-realized PowerTribe. I personally work with my clients through Phase One to be sure the business model is perfect, the revenue model is powerful, and the culture is a great fit. My staff work with you and your staff to get the system built, but I am always in the background monitoring progress.

I have the tools all defined, and the process details fully perfected. We work with clients and take them through the program in phases.

THE THREE PHASES TO CREATING AND LAUNCHING YOUR PROGRAM, AND HOW WE WORK TOGETHER

We spend several hours together on Skype/Zoom, and together we build the foundational documents and mind maps which show exactly how all the moving pieces fit together.

The process starts with understanding how a prospect and client (separately) flow through your marketing and sales/service systems. We look at each part of the process to see how having a Certified Consultant would benefit both the client and the company.

This helps you understand step-by-step when a new prospect enters your world, and where they become a client. This is important to know because we want to find a place where that client would interact with your CCs. It may be down the road, or it may be up front; regardless, these are parts of the decision-making process.

As an idea, imagine if you sold a training program for several thousand dollars. You have a return rate of 8-12%, and you know from experience that only a small portion of those who buy actually implement and follow through.

As it turns out, business owners are getting tired of putting one more training program on their virtual bookshelf and never reaping the benefits it should have delivered.

Envision this instead:

With each training program you sell, provide three, free, one-on-one coaching sessions to ensure your clients use the program and get up to speed properly. A percentage of those students will pay for ongoing coaching, as well.

If you had a Certified Coach program, those free coaching sessions can be delivered at no cost by your Certified Coach, who would welcome the lead flow and getting a chance to close more clients.

And, if you set up the coaching environment so your CCs could simply click one button and enroll students into their paid program, you can establish standard prices and share the revenue with your CCs. Everyone wins.

USE PHASE ONE TO CREATE ALL THE MARKETING, SELLING AND CERTIFICATION PLANS

The next step we take together is to plot the path an applicant will take as they move from being just interested to becoming a paid member of your program.

Just as I've detailed earlier in the book, we start with your launch sequence, step by step; then the application, then the interview, and finally, the acceptance of their application and payment for their enrollment. Looking back, it's pretty straightforward, but those details (and more) will provide a map of what we need to create inside the company that we may not already have.

We answer these questions:

» What about after they pay for their Certification Program?
» Do they sign a contract before they start their training?

This is where we make these types of Phase One decisions.

Let's be very clear about this. Every step in the sequence must be perfectly planned regarding what must be done, and exactly how to accomplish it.

This is your foundation, and it will serve you well to stay focused and get all the planning down up front. That is why I take you through the entire process, so no steps or pieces are missing.

We then design the back end (the special services and access) of the CC program and specify what we will need to accomplish Phase One. This will ultimately define the functionality we deliver to your PowerTribe.

For my clients, I provide the legal documents (as templates since I'm not a lawyer) for a Certified Consultant contract. This ensures that your intellectual property stays yours, and you don't risk them being classified as Independent Contractors by the state taxing authorities.

You can ask your attorney to create a contract for you and make sure your new Certified Consultant knows where they stand in terms of their relationship with the company and the scope of the system you are creating for them.

Next, we work out all of the profit splits and internal compensation levels for your Certified Consultants and the company. Decide all pricing of Certification and all the levels in your program in Phase One.

We stick with the mind map to identify every element of the work required, and every sales opportunity along the way that you can capitalize on. This will help organize our thoughts and keep track of every element of the program.

At the end of this phase, you will have a complete conceptual model of the whole program: the structural components, an estimate of the required tasks, work required, the general system requirements, and the projections for revenue through the first year. All this comes together in a summary document, which will show you every part of the entire program.

Next is the timeline for building each piece. We build this together; I will meet once a week with the team and take responsibility for keeping the program on track as everyone gets busy on other projects.

When I build this program along with my clients, I use a specific LMS system which conforms to all the required needs for Certification.

As previously mentioned, the system I use can be found here: http://tiny.cc/mitch. Their training shows you how to ensure your learning environment has maximum impact.

This system also has built-in tracking tools, so we know precisely where each student is along the way. The system will even send reminders (and notify management) if a student is absent more than a specified amount of time.

Next is the review of your entire launch sequence the development of the back-end CRM system you will use to track client engagement, and everything you need to enroll students.

Finally, we specify exactly what training materials, software, systems, infrastructure, management tools, staff, measurements, and control systems we will need for your whole program.

Phase One is over when your plan and your P/L is complete for your program.

Since many of you already have your intellectual property and training systems well-organized, I suspect you can complete the entire Certification Training environment in 30-45 days. If you have someone on staff who knows your content, you will have a very professional program when complete.

PHASE TWO STARTS WHEN YOU ARE DONE PLANNING AND READY TO BUILD.

In Phase Two, you will write and create everything you will need for your PowerTribe system to start. I provide templates for many of the items listed below:

What do you need?

» Sales Letters - We recommend three sales letters plus follow up.

» Sales Videos - This will follow the system I provided earlier in the book for exposing the problem and suggesting a solution, offering a total and complete business as the solution.

» Telephone Sales Scripts - For closing if you use sales people to screen applications, which is advisable.

» Learning Management System - Fully configured and ready for content.

» Your Content - 30 to 60 days of content for your training and Certification.

» Sales Funnel - Infusionsoft or other products to orchestrate the entire sales process.

» CRM System - For creating lead flow for your new CCs.

» Code of Ethics - A code that perfectly fits your company.

» Culture Training Program - A series of lessons to best communicate your Why and your Values.

» Graduation Certificates and Badges - Awarded at the end of training.

» Sales Training Program - For graduates who will need to learn to sell your system and their services.

» Program Manager - Identified and ready to start.

Phase Two ends when all these tasks are complete, when everything is tested and you know that people can flow through your entire system exactly as planned.

PHASE THREE IS WHEN YOU LAUNCH YOUR PROGRAM.

In Phase Three, you are beginning the launch sequence, and that should last until you fill your pilot class – usually 5-7 days, but with all the applications you will receive, you can leave it open for up to 10 days. As mentioned earlier, you can oversubscribe your pilot, because we know for certain that some small percentage of people who enrolled will drop out.

If you are employing a sales team to close on your applications, you will want to create a sales script and a training guide to ensure the maximum results are reached.

After you fill your class, the real work of training your PowerTribe class begins.

All throughout the training period, you will want to do extensive check-ins, mentoring, and coaching to make sure you understand where your new CCs are having problems understanding the material. After you coach them, fix the training. Let this be as real-time as possible. Your goal is to use the pilot program to fix anything that wasn't perfect the first time through.

After your pilot class graduates, you are ready to help them be successful. This is where it gets real for all the participants in the program, and for your company, as well.

I work with your Program Manager to make sure they have what they need to support your program before, during, and after the applications close.

YOUR LEAD GENERATION PROGRAM

Leads are what drive your program forward, what makes you different from others who offer Certification; this is also what causes people to re-certify the following year. Leads are the lifeblood of any company, and for your PowerTribe, you will need to provide enough leads for each person to close a deal in their first 30-60 days.

Your best leads come from your prospect list. No matter how old that list is, you can reignite their interest with a more powerful proposition. Instead of simply buying your program, you can now offer it along with three or four free coaching sessions. Those free sessions are a great motivator to get deals closed and create new clients for both your company AND your new PowerTribe.

After your CCs are in the field, your job is to make them successful. Continue to follow up constantly so that everyone can become a success. The more CCs that are successful in this phase, the better your chances are of recruiting an enthusiastic second, third, fourth, etc., and graduating a new class every quarter.

As the group starts to build, you many need to hire a leadership person who can run the program with a daily "boots on the ground" responsibility-monitoring plan. They will solely be running the program and handling the needs of CCs.

By working with my company, your chances of success will be far greater, and the time to delivery will be much shorter. Yes, it's somewhat expensive; but in general, fees are recovered within 7 days of launching your pilot class, and then you have a lifetime to continuously build your recurring revenue empire.

Like all things in life, you can accelerate this process by working with an expert. In this book, I have held nothing back; and if you follow the blueprint chapter, reinforced by the specific information about each step, then you can do it on your own.

In the end, the goal is to have a powerful, scalable program to support your dreams, your aspirations, and your goals for many years to come. Do it; it's worth it!

CHAPTER SIXTEEN

WHAT CAN GO WRONG?

POOR PLANNING AND GREED NEVER SUCCEED

RECENTLY, I RECEIVED A SKYPE MESSAGE from a CEO who I greatly admired. They had created a powerful system for helping people and companies discover their true mission. It was so transformative that just the promise alone was enough to get coaches very interested in learning the system.

The CEOs started to add coaches to their company because they discovered that they would pay for Certification. They exploited coaches as a source of revenue instead of focusing on adding true partners to their business. They made promises to their coaching network they could not keep, charged prices that were too high for most to recover, and never truly built the type of support system for the company that a Consultant/Coaching network is supposed to be.

Needless to say, they were in trouble, and I was asked to help. In less than a week, I had interviewed all their staff and discovered what some of the core problems were, as well as what it was that drove some of their original thoughts.

Unfortunately, they had made the classic mistake when trying to build a certified coaching division: they put themselves first.

In life, and in business, this is rarely the best way to play with others. In every interaction, our goal is to put our partners' needs first and support their most precious resources: vendors, coaches, consultants, and trainers.

There was only one logical way out for my new client: abandon the current model and rebuild it with the right core values. Unfortunately, that was not the most viable option, for their company would collapse from the loss of Certification fees.

I had to first come up with a plan to fix their program, with a clear, powerful business model that was more inclusive of their Coaches than ever before and that would make it thrive into the powerful support system their Coaches were craving.

There was no doubt about the power of their transformative process, which changed lives and companies; it was the way Coaches were treated and later abused that caused the majority of their problems.

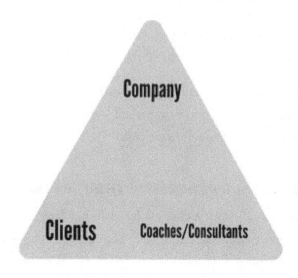

To do that, I first needed to make sure the fundamental requirements for a powerful, functioning network would be in place. Without this, there would be no chance of fixing their current network or starting from scratch the right way.

In either case, I required that the same core values I shared with you earlier, with one critical driving force:

This must be a win for clients, a win for their coaches, and a win for the company.

As you can see from the above triangle, if any one of those three corners drop, the whole triangle falls apart. There is a balance, and they had violated that balance.

If they put the company first, there is no doubt that the other two parts of the equation would never be fully established.

You could say this all sounds like a grand idea but is no longer applicable. But you would be mistaken if you did.

Today, PowerTribes are more connected to their sponsoring company than ever before, creating an intimate link – a critically important element in every PowerTribe network.

Without that link, your tribe won't work; you won't sell Certification, and the company will lose sight of the value they might have received.

You have to create a completed business plan before you start and work to discover all the potential pitfalls before there are live souls in your program expecting so much from you.

BUILDING YOUR PROGRAM WITHOUT A PLAN

I received a call from a client – let's call her Jane – who found herself in exactly that place. She had a very popular women's book that led her clients to form powerful, bonding love relationships with their spouses. It was a breakthrough process, and she was smart enough to know how to leverage that book into an entire business. Her company was helping women achieve their dreams, but the need for individual help created both an opportunity and a potential problem.

Unfortunately, she didn't have a plan; she simply started to position people as coaches and help get them clients. Some were readers of her book; others were friends who she thought she would enjoy working with. While it was a great idea in theory, it wasn't well planned, and it caused disastrous problems.

There was one point in time where she felt like she was losing control of her outside coaches. One coach actually copied her intellectual property to their own website and represented it as her own. Another coach was incompetent, yet my client didn't know how to handle this effectively.

When I came along, she was desperate and needed someone to untangle the mess she was in. She needed to get everything working again.

It took me only one month to completely "fix" her coaching organization and get her reoriented into a place where her coaches were an asset instead of a liability. Before I could do anything, I had to understand her business, the problems she had, and the people she was working with. This took a little while, but when I had a handle on this, I was able to apply most of the same techniques I used as CEO of Timeslips and many of the concepts in this book.

I did that by simply putting into place some rules (I called this "the Code of Ethics"), which were the internal rules the company would abide by regarding how we treat clients, staff, and coaches. We also brought in some legal templates I had created for her with my lawyer. The agreements included some training processes that ensured 100% comprehension of their most valuable information.

Now they were ready to rock! And they did, smoothly doubling in revenue over the following year.

WHY DO POWERTRIBES FAIL?

This is, thankfully, an obvious answer, which you can prevent with your own PowerTribe by paying attention and doing what you promise.

First of all, make sure your training is the best if can be. It's no trivial matter to create a learning management system for your topic, but if you follow the guideline in this book, you will get pretty darn close even if you've never done it before.

If you're the company owner, and you are building this organization, spend time nurturing it. Call members and chat; meet them for group dinners when you travel; make them feel they are important to you. And they will be, guaranteed.

In one case, one of my CCs rewrote our software manual to make it easier to read; another volunteered to create the Spanish version for us at no charge. Why do people do this without asking for money? They want to be admired by important people, and they want to be recognized by their peers.

Clearly to some, these things are more important than money; but the lesson I've learned is: don't accept work for free. Always pay for the work you want to be done. If you don't, you are setting yourself up for a problem down the road because everyone else is watching how you handle the situation, and eventually those same people may feel used or abused.

This goes back to building your culture deliberately.

Be aware of one other factor: jealousy.

With my software company, Timeslips Corp., a few of our CCs stood out as the most helpful, most loyal, and most enthusiastic of all. They had their own reasons, but being a new CEO, I simply accepted their offers to assist. Before long, several were working on projects they had volunteered to take on. We never discussed pay or any remuneration for their services; they just seemed as if they wanted to help. So, I let them. Being focused more on my goals than on theirs, I let them help – too much. So much so that a few of them felt resentful of all the work they were doing without being rewarded.

I don't blame them. I blame myself for not having the foresight to see what I was creating by letting them work that way. This came from my lack of experience, which I paid the penalty for many times over. You can learn from my mistakes and be very careful about this. It's so important to stress that you always have to remember your CCs are watching your daily actions and behavior to discern how you will treat them.

I created a chasm between those elite few and the rest of the group. Worse, those who were NOT in that elite group now began feeling resentful for the favoritism. I should have known better, but how could I have? I was simply inexperienced, and maybe a little "entitled" at the same time. At one point, the resentment in at least one individual built up so badly that he attacked the company in a destructive way. I had to call the police. But it never should have gone that far.

I'm explaining this in detail now so you don't make the same mistake. It's very easy to let this happen, but you had better not, or you may find yourself in a bad situation.

Here are a few thoughts about how to work with your CCs as your team builds:

If you find that one or more Certified Consultants step up to take on an additional responsibility, welcome them, but document what you expect from them. Offer to pay them for their time, and when they deliver, pay them promptly. You can also offer them a quid pro quo, such as a premium spot at your next event or a feature on your website. Always memorialize your agreements in advance of accepting any work.

If those that step up out of the kindness of their heart are not qualified to do so, thank them and offer to help them get qualified. No one likes to feel rejected, so find a way to help them instead.

When a CC offers to appear at an event or a public appearance, make the relationship clear and explain what they can and cannot do. If they show up, they'll want to sell their services, and usually, that's a good thing. But you may not want them to. So explain that they don't have to come, but if they do, there is no solicitation of services while they are there, if that's your policy. Ask them to sign an agreement stating exactly what is and what is not allowed, and make sure everyone has signed one before they are allowed into the meeting area.

Tony Robbins has a whole team of volunteers that attends his events. Tony's volunteers work pretty hard; they know they shouldn't solicit. They love Tony and want to be near him, and they want to do whatever is necessary. But don't think volunteers can just do whatever they want. If they sign up to be a volunteer, they must follow the direction of the program manager, who makes sure they all have responsibilities.

That's all well and good, as long as it's defined in advance, an agreement is signed, and everyone knows what to expect. As a "gift" for volunteering, Tony spends some private time with the volunteers to make sure they feel loved, and they do.

They also get to listen in on the valuable programs that Tony teaches during his events. That's part of the deal – enjoying the benefits as if they had paid for them – but their "job" as volunteers comes first. Only after they complete their work are they allowed to enjoy the presentations.

CHAPTER SEVENTEEN

MARKETING PROGRAMS TO SUPPORT YOUR NEW TRIBE

GENERATING LEADS FOR YOUR CERTIFIED CONSULTANTS:

O NE OF THE MOST IMPORTANT differentiators of your program will be your ability to provide lead flow for your Certified Consultants. Doing so sets you apart and makes your program far more attractive. At the time you recruited your Certified Consultants, they may have already evaluated other business opportunities and turned those down. Why is your program different? Besides the core mission of your company, it will most certainly be because you provide all the components of a Consulting/Coaching business and solve the single largest problem all Coaches and Consultants face. Providing leads is the difference between your program and the others who don't.

Great Coaches and Consultants sometimes aren't great salespeople, and rarely great marketers. If they were, they would already be in business building their own coaching organization. Their biggest problem is acquiring prospects and converting them into clients, which is why our lead flow program is so valuable. Our job is to provide prospect flow and then training on conversion into a sale.

Take this into account when you set the price for your program. Understand that marketing will cost money, and that by allocating funds on a per-Certified-Consultant basis, you will be able to spend what you need to generate leads for your Tribe.

If you bring 20 people into your pilot class and charge $20,000 per seat, that generates $400,000 just from admission alone. If you take 20% of this and use it to generate leads for your Certified Consultants, they will succeed.

CREATING THE ASSESSMENT:

I have found that an assessment works great at generating leads from a prospect base. If this were for existing prospects, the questions would be different than for new prospects. Build a dynamic assessment, invite people to come fill that out, and offer a free consultation with a Certified Consultant. It's a great way to show value up front and can be used with many of the techniques listed below.

You can download an example of an assessment by going to PowerTribesBook.com/assessment

Let's take a look at some other ways we can generate leads for a Certified Consultant:

YOUR EXISTING DATABASE:

Think about all of the leads that you've accumulated over the years and did not convert into sales. Now imagine you put all of those leads into a fresh auto-responder program and warm them up using a new approach. Let them know that there are now Certified Consultants in their area who they can use to help build their company!

Most of the companies I know don't follow up on enough on the leads they already get. If you fall into that category, what better way to follow-up then by using your PowerTribe. Your Certified Consultants will thank you, you'll generate more revenue for your company at the same time, and those leads are virtually free; no cost of acquisition because you already have them, anyway.

PAID ADVERTISING:

What about paid ads? Have you run Facebook ads, Google ad words, or have you been promoting on LinkedIn? All of those are great sources of leads for your Certified Consultants. There are several companies that you can hire who will generate leads or set up automated lead generation systems for you. If we allocate 20% of the amount we collected in Certification fees, that would mean we had $80,000 a year to generate leads for twenty Certified Consultants. That's around $6,666 in lead generation budget per month.

CO-OP ADVERTISING:

This next idea is an advanced technique that I've used successfully several times. It's advanced because it takes a bit of setup to make it work. It's called co-op advertising. The idea behind this is to create promotional activities for Certified Consultants who pay extra to be included in this special program. All leads are shared equally with each participant. In involves running radio ads in regions or nationally, then feeding the resulting calls into a phone tree, which rings each participant in order so everyone gets an even share of the leads. As each prospect calls in, they are sent to a different Certified Consultant who'll answer the phone and work with the client to help them with what they need.

At one point, we had about 50 people a month in our co-op program; it continued for a long time until the radio station raised their rates, which made the program undesirable. You can do this with Facebook ads; Google ad words, anything that generates leads, but only for those

Certified Consultants who pay extra to share in the lead flow. To put this in perspective, it didn't cost more than $300 a month per Certified Consultant to be included in the lead pool, yet everyone received between 5 and 10 new leads a week.

RADIO:

Once your Certified Consultant network starts to reach between 50 and 80 people, consider using the radio to bring in leads. I wrote about radio extensively in my first book, *The Invisible Organization*. In that book, I highlighted how most people think radio is only for big advertisers. Radio is fantastic for small businesses, particularly when they want to reach local customers. If you sell nationally, you can create a successful radio ad and run it nationwide on Sirius XM for about the same amount of money you would spend on local ads and get coverage in all 50 states with ease.

JOINT VENTURES:

Then, of course, consider the power of joint ventures. With the JV model, you could work with other companies and introduce their products through your Certified Consultants in exchange for having them promote you and your Certified Consultants to their own network. When I was in the software business, we worked with three other software companies that gave us access collectively to an entire vertical market. Just by having Certified Consultants, my company was in the center of all that activity. As an additional benefit, I had negotiated linking our software to theirs as a requirement to use our Certified Consultants to promote their products. That was a great arrangement which gives me access to their entire customer base, with their help promoting me.

LOCAL PUBLIC RELATIONS:

One other very effective way of generating activity for Certified Consultants is to use local public relations. When I work with my clients, I recommend hiring a part-time P/R intern who works locally for each Certified Consultant to find local bar association meetings, CPA association meetings, Business Roundtable meetings, and, in some cases, Vistage meetings as well. The gratitude from doing this just one or two times will pay many dividends tenfold. The presence you have in all 50 states gives you an edge over your competitors even if you are not the dominant player in your marketplace.

COMPANY TRAVEL PLANS:

Remember that no matter where your personnel are on a day-to-day basis, you should always include Certified Consultants in your travel plans. If you're going on a business trip, always set aside one extra evening and meet with your local Certified Consultants; buy them dinner and let them talk. They will have lots of suggestions to improve the program, and they will appreciate the time you spent in a very big way. When I traveled the country for my software company, I made a point of doing this on every single business trip. I got to know many of these Certified Consultants personally, and they stayed friends for many years. It's easy to do, it's fun, it's informative, and it builds the culture like nothing else I can imagine.

TRADE SHOWS:

Naturally, the same idea it extends to trade shows or other public events that your company hosts or attends. I know that when we appeared at COMDEX many years ago, our booth was staffed by several Certified Consultants every day. I was thrilled when I saw them talking to customers and setting up appointments to discuss how Timeslips can could help them in their business. I couldn't have paid for better staff even if I wanted to. The way I rewarded them was to cover lodging and meals. Naturally, I took them all to dinner several times during that week to show my appreciation.

One of my clients provides their Certified Consultants with table displays. Their Certified Consultants use them at "lunch and learns" where they can reach several dozen prospects or more in corporate cafeterias.

WEBSITE:

One other important way to market your Certified Consultants is to include them in your marketing materials. Talk about having this nationwide presence on your website. When you communicate with your clients at any level, make sure to mention your nationwide force of Certification partners. This will benefit the company in so many ways. It sets you up as a leader in your field, and it sets you apart from all of your competitors.

I have been asked about creating directories of Certified Consultants, and in the past, I have not done so because I didn't want other companies soliciting all of my Certified Consultants. Instead, we built a zip code look-up page, so anyone needing a Certified Consultant could see only a few who were in their area.

Build a website template for your CCs and distribute it for free, or host it on a shared server. This way, you get to control the content and leave them specific areas to customize. Your PowerTribe will be grateful. This is one of those key elements that brings back your Certified Consultants to the program every year, and it costs very little to host.

RETAIL PRESENTATIONS:

Depending on your products and services, you can also send your Certified Consultants to retail locations to talk to customers at a shop. We did this successfully in Staples and Egghead Discount Software. In many cases, people stopped to talk about our software when they noticed that a representative from the company was in the store. This was amazingly successful at getting assignments for our Certified Consultants.

Another one of my clients does a full-blown company rollout at the main headquarters with each new client they sign. They invite their Certified Consultants to every rollout as a learning experience, to see exactly how it's done. As the company got busier, they began to rely more and more on their Certified Consultants to assist with their rollouts. Eventually, the goal is to take the CEO off the road and let her focus on building the business instead of showing up at every customer rollout.

WEBINARS:

Another powerful promotional tool is the webinar template. Arm your Certified Consultants with pre-recorded webinars that they can run on their own. As the webinar plays, they can answer questions that come in through chat. The webinar can be built specifically to focus on the value Certified Consultants bring to the product and on the service your company offers. This allows your more ambitious Certified Consultants to take better control of their own marketing. Obviously, if your product is less oriented to share in a webinar environment, substitute other equivalent means.

We want to encourage our Certified Consultants to do their own marketing. We need to give them marketing materials they can use in multiple ways, any way they see fit. In my company, I provided the correspondence that was required to book a client, including all the correspondence that followed a client engagement. I did this when I found out that my Certified Consultants were not following up and were looking unprofessional, making us look unprofessional as well.

BUILDING CRM INTO YOUR BACK END:

As I am sure you know, CRM is Customer Relationship Management software used to stay in front of your prospects. There's no reason why you can't do the same thing for your CCs. Why not set up an auto-responder with all of the emails that would follow, promoting a successful visit to a local company? Allow the CRM auto-responder to do all the work and prompt your Certified Consultant to follow-up at various intervals. The more tools you give your Certified Consultants for marketing, the more marketing they will do, and the more sales and revenue you will generate for everyone.

LIVE FORUM FOR YOUR CERTIFIED CONSULTANTS:

Because all of your Certified Consultants will be able to interact in a live forum, such as a Facebook private group, encourage them to share marketing ideas as well. Let them post successful campaigns they have used that others in noncompetitive areas could use, too. You can even set up a contest to see who can create the best marketing material and award a prize for the winner.

CONTESTS:

Speaking of contests, we ran them often. Internally we had a contest for support technicians who generated the most testimonial letters. You can do the same thing with your Certified Consultants, giving them an incentive to collect testimonials from their clients and publicly celebrate the ones who do. Teach them to ask for referrals from every successful engagement. Pay bonuses, send gift cards, even vacation certificates or other electronic gifts for doing a great job. Nothing works better then appreciation!

The more attention you show your Certified Consultants by helping them succeed, the more revenue you'll generate for everyone. Never think of your Certified Consultants as overhead; instead, think of them as assets. If you treat your assets well, they will appreciate and value you; if you don't, well, you know what happens.

Everything I've shared with you in this chapter should be a beginning. Use it to jumpstart your program and discover more ways to generate leads for your Certified Consultants. Only good things come from helping those who depend on you to build their business.

CHAPTER EIGHTEEN

HOW THIS WORKS IN THE REAL WORLD

LET'S TAKE A CLOSE LOOK at a medical device company that sells a tool to dentists, which consists of installing an appliance in the patient's mouth. Let's call him Dr. Robertson.

Dr. Robertson had graduated school as a dentist but was an inventor at heart. Dr. Robertson grew his adolescent practice and enjoyed working with teens and those who needed braces. He noticed that braces were ugly and that they were almost a rite of passage for teens that most would rather do without.

One day, while solving a problem in a young man's dental appliance, he noticed that by structuring the appliance with some self-tightening wires, he was able to shorten the time it took for his clients to straighten their teeth. Teens were thrilled, and moms rejoiced at having to spend fewer trips to the dentist, as well.

The only problem was that the mechanism in the appliance required a special fitting, and without the training, most dentists wouldn't know how to properly install it. Robert could not just sell these devices; the dentists had to be trained on how to install them. However, if installed properly, it would save the dentist from a lengthy trial and error period, significantly speed up the healing cycle with patients, and deliver better results.

Dr. Robertson traveled to local meetings and demonstrated his patented invention but understood that they would need proper training before implementing his tool.

Eventually, he started a company around this idea and decided to "certify" dentists so that they would be licensed to use his product.

Once a year, the company held their national meeting where dentists would come for three days of training, but not everyone would show up. The dentists who failed show up not only lost out on valuable information, but they lost their Certification, as well. Some chose never to buy because of this training requirement.

The company was losing clients (dentists) and losing market share while less intrusive but less effective systems came into the marketplace. These systems were favorable mainly because they didn't require dentists to travel every year.

Using the concept of a PowerTribe, Robert saw the value in shifting his model to the one documented in this book and decided to make some immediate changes. He realized that he could easily deploy several hundred Certified Consultants who would have a support territory for helping dentists in their offices, which alleviated the need for dentists to travel. The dentists watched video training, and then afterward would contact a CC to supervise, guide, and inspect the doctor's work with their first few patients.

You can imagine what an astounding revenue opportunity this was for the CC network, and what an incredible savings of expenses it was for Robert.

LET'S TAKE A CLOSER LOOK AT JUST WHAT HAPPENED.

Dr. Robertson solicited other dentists, who were very interested in becoming "Certified," to help local dentists for a fee. He then set a very high price for certification and required yearly re-certification to stay in the program. Then, as his company grew and introduced new products, his CC program became the launch pad for penetrating thousands of dental offices in a short period.

HERE'S HOW DR. ROBERTSON MADE MONEY:

» The dental appliance was sold directly to dentists for a fixed fee.

» The company sold certification to local dentists who wanted to work outside their office for a fixed fee.

» The company then gathered all their Certified Dentists together once a year for a symposium and charged a hefty fee to attend.

» The company added a kit of supplies that every dentist's office should have for fixing and adjusting the appliance in their patient's mouth.

» The CEO realized that some of his Certified Dentists were interested in helping sign up new dentists, so he built a sales training program and charged for admission.

» The CEO also realized that not all dentists would step up, so he built another level called Mentor Dentists. He charged for this level as well and added an additional level of testing.

» The company now trains everyone to be Certified remotely and assigns them to Mentors who make money for each Dentist they mentor.

And on and on.

We named seven revenue sources that appeared out of thin air to make Dr. Robertson a very wealthy man in three short years, all from following the simple blueprint in this book. He now had a very valuable asset he wanted to ensure he built with care. He also wanted to ensure the safety of his patent and his processes by using the legal templates I provide for my clients.

I hope you see now how this all fits together.

CHAPTER NINTEEN

MULTIPLE STREAMS OF RECURRING REVENUE

WHAT DO THE FINANCIALS LOOK LIKE AFTER THE PILOT?

I T'S NOW TIME TO DO THE ANALYSIS and see if, financially, it was rewarding to launch our Pilot CC Program. This can help us determine how and when we will do it again.

When we started, we needed to decide what we would charge for applicants to join our program. For my clients, I've seen fees ranging from $6,000 to $28,000 per applicant. We must deliver an opportunity that can perform 3x - 10x that fee if our applicants are to sign up. If not, then figure out how it can or lower your fees.

All the programs I design are designed to enroll CCs for one year only. This means that CCs get the training and are included in the program for a year, all for their original Pilot Fee. Since it's a pilot, it is implied, and should be clear, that future applicants will pay more. This means that as new people sign up, their application fee will go up by 30-50%. Also, their "year" begins when they graduate, not when they start their training.

Let's use my client's $6,000 application fee as an example. In this case, he chose to run his Pilot Program a little bigger than I recommend because he had the support staff to handle that many people and get them through the course. I mentioned earlier that we like to have about 20 people in a pilot – maybe a few more to cover those who drop out early.

With 18 people paying on average $6,000, he netted $108,000. Let's say it takes three months to get everyone through the pilot, fix all the mistakes in our initial program, and get enough testimonials to help sell the next class; then we are ready to multiply our growth.

Also assume the new price goes from $6,000 to $8,000, and the number of people he closes registration with is 20. I believe that's conservative, but it's a start. That means the next class generates $160,000 in application fees.

60 days later, he does it again and now gets 25 people to join; that's an additional $200,000, with a total of $468,000 for the first year over what that company would have made without their CC Program.

It's easy to see how we can run this program as an "evergreen," meaning that once the launch videos and funnels are built, it can almost run on automatic over and over again, generating more signups into the program on a continuous basis.

Let's be conservative and say that the following year, we get another 25 graduates every quarter, and we don't raise the price. That means we generate $800,000 in application fees alone. But what about the graduates from last year?

We have, conservatively, about 65 people who are still working as CCs in our program. They wouldn't be still working if it were not making them money, so they are happy to renew their Certification. Let's say we charge $5K for recertification, which, again, I think is conservative. That's another $325,000 in Year Two from Year One students. That brings our program to $1,125,000 in revenue in Year Two.

And we are only just getting started.

Now, let's run a symposium at the end of Year Two, and we charge just $999 to attend. But, we up-sell VIP status at $395, and half of the group buys it. Let's say we get just 100 people to attend this year. That comes to roughly $119,000 to run a symposium at a hotel somewhere in Las Vegas, or wherever you think it works well to have an event.

When they get to the event, you keep everyone excited by showing them new features, training them on some of the techniques they can use to grow their business, and present awards to the top earning CCs. In this event, we also introduce the idea of a certain number of CCs upgrading from their current status (let's use the term: Apprentices) to become Mentors.

What is a Mentor?

A Mentor is someone who can take 8-12 new graduates from the program under their wing and get them to generate successful client assignments faster than if they did it themselves. Let's say we sell Mentorship for $35K and show how it can generate an additional $100K for each Mentor.

Mentors take 15% - 25% of the Apprentices fees while under Mentorship. Simply put, the Apprentice pays the Mentor for his help. The Mentor answers questions, debugs client problems, helps with execution, and overall acts as an advisor to the Apprentice.

Follow me so far?

Let's say we limit this to just 5 Mentors in Year One. That's another $175K (and I am using smaller, conservative numbers to make a point), and now we are up to $294K for our event. At the event, we introduce a new product. It's a higher-end product that greatly benefits our clients and will become another consulting opportunity down the road.

Let's also sell discounted admission to next year's symposium Finally, at the end of the event, we explain that next year's event is going to be double the price, but everyone here can get in next year for the same price as this year, just $999. So, another 50% of the room enrolls on the spot.

Now, we are up $344K in revenue for this very first CC event for our company.

Our investment?

Four days of our time plus some expenses at the hotel. The biggest expense may be the film crew who was filming all the presentations so that they can be made into products for the following year.

COMPANY GROWTH:

Think about where you will be at the end of Year Two with 150 Certified Consultants. What will be the tangential effects of having those beautiful people in the field, all helping you be successful as they become successful in their own right?

At Timeslips Corp., many years ago, our CC population was responsible for nearly 20% of our revenue. Sometimes, we never knew how much they promoted and sold our products through other channels. They sold product directly and indirectly, which grew our bottom line.

They also reduced our support expense as their work offset our own Tech Support Department, which clients would call all too often. The CC could then use those opportunities to sign clients of their own, and we loved it!

Think hard about what you have just read:

» What does that mean to you?

» Will you see more sales?

» Will you sell more products?

» More add-ons?

» What other ways can your CCs generate revenue for your company?

Remember, this example is based on a very low number to start with. If you charge more for certification, and you have a large base to draw from, your numbers can be substantially larger.

For a full walkthrough of a prospective set of financials for this program, go to PowerTribesBook.com/assessment.

CHAPTER TWENTY

WE LAUNCHED. NOW WHAT?

WE LAUNCHED OUR PILOT; WHAT'S NEXT?

CONGRATULATIONS, YOU MADE IT THROUGH! You have a fully functional pilot class of students who are out there in the world working to sell and support your products and your company. Without a doubt, this is the most powerful business tactic I've seen that pays you back as fast as it does. It probably didn't cost you too much to build your program; or if you used someone to orchestrate and project-manage this process, any fees you paid should be fully reimbursed in the first week of your program. So essentially, it's free after the first week of launch, and then it will be streaming profits for the rest of your business life.

Now that the pilot is launched, there's still so much to do. Our goal is to make the next launch go as smoothly as possible, and that means we must constantly be monitoring the progress of the students in our pilot program.

The process is new, it has been given a lot of thought, and if you followed the steps in this book carefully and completely, then you probably have most of it fairly close to perfect. It's that last 3% that makes the difference for most companies; it's that last 3% we want to get right, so it doesn't consume 97% of our time the next time through.

Here's another reason to stay super focused on this process right now and to make sure you get it right:

If you do, you can "evergreen" your next launch, as I mentioned earlier, running it on automatic and having non-contiguous classes. This means you can have people starting anytime, and graduates will stream through without a particular group to call the "graduating class." If you do this, make sure you can handle the number of people who are moving through the program without dropping the level of support or service. This ensures that the quality of your graduates never varies.

Most people, after having a successful pilot, move directly into the post-mortem phase, which means we are now going to dissect the sticking points and smooth them out. Some of these sticky points include, but are not limited to:

» Correcting everything that went wrong;

» Fixing lessons that require too much follow-up or correction;

» Everything that caused questions from our students that our automated training should have answered;

» Any objections that came up, as well;

» Find those things we didn't teach but that they needed after graduating, and add them.

The more work you put into the post-mortem phase, the less work you will have each time you do this. And, following this process of doing a post-mortem after every launch, you will eventually reduce all problems and issues to nearly zero.

Even now, after your second launch, you have more to do if you want to fully realize the profit potential of this incredible machine!

STAFFING YOUR PROGRAM

When I founded Timeslips Corporation, I wanted to know exactly how this program would evolve, and I wanted to make sure it received a lot of my personal attention. As a result of wanting to be so hands-on, I worked closely with an administrator to execute some of the details I wanted to have done, and I made all the decisions myself, involving the admin along the way.

Over time, she went from overwhelmed to self-sufficiency, and I was checking in daily to see if there were any issues she had that needed my attention. In about four months, I stopped the daily meetings, added her to my weekly management meeting, and she became the Program Director for the CC Program.

Two wonderful things happened: she became a respected member of the management team, and she kept adding incremental improvements all along the way. As large as my PowerTribe was, it never required more than one person to manage. The exception was our live symposiums. This was an "all hands on deck" situation, and for most of the staff, it was a huge treat to be out at our event, interacting with our CCs and making those personal connections with people who have been only phone relationships up until then.

When you have a well-designed program, executed carefully to deliver a highly- qualified Consultant or Coach or Counselor, you won't need a lot of program management. Having a well-designed online resource for your PowerTribe to access and a help system for them to interact with will go a long way to making your program manager a happier person.

When it comes to online forums, I highly recommend that if you set them up, you always monitor their activity. Sometimes these types of environments can be damaging based on incorrect or misunderstood information. Participate as personally as possible to stem any negative speech, and deal with real issues head-on. Forthright honesty and deliberate action are the most powerful ways to handle any problems that do surface. Just do it quickly, so it doesn't get ahead of you.

CHAPTER TWENTY-ONE

YEAR TWO AND YEAR THREE OF YOUR PROGRAM

THE HARD WORK IS DONE

Imagine now that you have twelve sticks and twelve plates, and your objective is to get all twelve plates spinning on all twelve sticks. Clearly, it's harder to get that started than it is to maintain the momentum. In this phase of your program, you goal and mission is to maintain and build momentum.

THE 3 KEY ELEMENTS OF MOMENTUM IN YOUR POWERTRIBE.

The first element of momentum is your support. If your internal support systems for your Certified Consultants is superb, if their questions are answered quickly, and if you've already put out several fires and saved their "bacon," as it were, then your support will be literally legendary. The things you do to contribute to your CCs' lives and living will become either legends or horror stories that are passed on from generation to another.

Here's an example: One of my own CCs went to a client engagement and trained the entire staff at my client's company. At the end of the training, the staff was confused, and the CC left abruptly and was rude about being told the training was ineffective. I jumped right in, paid another CC to go over to that office and retrain those people to perfection, and I was a hero. The CC who flubbed the assignment was suspended until they were retrained and recertified, and that story was told repeatedly. That's what it means to be a legend in your own company.

It's your values that shine through every experience.

The second element of momentum is your attention. The more attention you give your PowerTribe, the faster it will grow and thrive. Remember when your relationship with your spouse was young and you spent every waking minute thinking about them, and when you saw each other that thirst was quenched? Later in life, you may not even notice her unless she asks you a question. That's how most people ruin good PowerTribes, and good marriages. They ignore them until they start getting bad, and then they pay the wrong type of attention.

I am not a marriage counselor, but I do know a thing or two about building these programs, and they need a lot of attention. If you PowerTribe is not hearing from YOU, the CEO, at least once a week, then you are asking for trouble. If you Program Manager is not calling them individually at least every 60 days, you won't be happy with the outcome. If you can do a monthly check-in call, even better.

The point here is that this group needs to feel connected to you and to your company. They need to see you expressing your "Why" in everything you do.

Traveling to a city on business? Invite your CCs. Having a regional presentation? Invite your CCs. Announcing a new product or service?

Make sure your CCs know about it a month in advance and have been trained to both up-sell it and deliver it.

Your CCs should be like an extension of your family. If you treat them with love and respect, they will throw gobs of money at you in the form of new orders, updates and upgrades, regional and local presentations on your behalf, articles and blog posts – all in admiration of the one company that they have pledged their allegiance to AND that has pledged its allegiance to them.

Need a Consultant to do something for the company? If it is a fit, hire one of your CCs first, pay a fair amount, and never take something for free, even if it's offered. The result will be powerful, visible, and worthwhile.

The third element of momentum is lead flow. It's all about how you help grow their business; it brings them back year after year, renewal after renewal, symposium after symposium – you are building their business alongside them.

I mentioned this earlier but can't stress it enough: Go out of your way to generate business for your CCs and the flow will reverse itself tenfold. Here are a few reminders:

Hire an intern to call bar associations, accountancy groups, and research meet-ups in every area where you have a Certified Consultant and arrange to have them present on behalf of the company, where they can pick up new clients.

Build a website template they can customize for all your CCs and host it as part of their yearly fee. This is just one more example of making it too compelling to leave if they ever have a change of heart.

Create monthly training sessions to improve their skills is sales, communication, marketing, Facebook advertising, blogging – anything that will help them grow their business.

Create a profile on all your CCs, know what their specialties are, and make introductions from time to time; it will ripple through the community and everyone will know.

Give them templates for their business cards and letterheads name them as a Certified Consultant and arrange bulk printing at a discount so they can buy their own cards. Better yet, buy their cards for them so you can further control what they use as their title and how your brand is represented. It may cost all of $20 per person, and it is worth it.

Send holiday cards, including little gifts like $10 Starbucks gift cards just to continue to show appreciation. One year, I sent everyone a $5 McDonald's Gift Card. Everyone on staff told me no one eats at McDonalds anymore, yet it was one of the holiday gifts that was for some reason most appreciated. Go figure! Just send something to show you are thinking of them and they will feel appreciated!

Those "Three Elements of Momentum" – your support, your attention, and lead flow – will keep your PowerTribe in love with you for many years to come.

You are in this for the long haul. True, the cash flow happens quickly, but the real wealth comes over the years as your network continues to grow. Your PowerTribe will become one of your greatest assets and will double and triple the value of your company while clearing the playing field when it comes to your competition.

This is your game changer; make it happen and evolve your company into the future.

SUMMARY

You hold in your hands, or on your Kindle, the entire blueprint for success. This business model is unusual – it's hard to get right and it takes a while to prepare – but if you follow the model I've laid out for you, it's almost guaranteed to succeed.

If I can be of help along the way, reach out and let's talk; I am always willing to help someone who's taking the risk and the time to grow their company.

Sincerely,

Mitch Russo

Mitch@mitchrusso.com

MyPowerTribe.com

ABOUT THE AUTHOR

A S A CHILD, I WAS A NEW YORK CITY street kid with a flair for adventure. At age twelve my friends and I would cut class on Thursdays and travel by subway to Coney Island, taking advantage of the two-for-one special on all the rides.

At age thirteen, I had my first minimum-wage job assembling black lights at a hippie poster store in Greenwich Village. When I was sixteen, my rock band played gigs at frat parties and Sweet Sixteen's, even the occasional political conventions.

Unfortunately, my "flair for adventure" eventually got me in trouble: I dropped out of high school and became addicted to heroin at age sixteen. After eighteen months I completed a resident rehab program and was determined to stay healthy and become successful.

I finished high school and enrolled in the DeVry Technical Institute to learn how to fix color TVs. Thanks to the passionate interest of one professor who saw something special in me, I became enthralled with digital electronics and computers.

After graduation, I was lured into an entry-level position at a Massachusetts computer company by a beauty-queen/recruiter who traveled to trade schools looking for recent grads to hire, promising the moon. Shortly afterwards I found myself on the nightshift assembling computer frames at Data General, bored and angry that I was duped into moving from NYC to rural Massachusetts. Fortunately, an influential engineer took a liking to me and realized that I had more potential. He made a phone call and arranged an interview with Digital Equipment Corp (DEC) in the R&D labs.

After four grueling hours of interviews, I got the job. I was very excited. Mr. Bill Angel was the key developer of a new technology – he was using dynamic ram chips to build the memory sub-system for the new VAX 11-780, and I was his junior engineer. The world was hungry for this cutting-edge technology, which would allow the increase of the size of the available usable memory without adding pins to each integrated circuit or changing the printed circuit board layout. The odds were against us. The chips were new, the technology buggy, and we were novices, but we succeeded! When the VAX was shipped in 1978, it had our memory boards inside.

Years later, the CEO of a major security company offered me an incredible opportunity when he asked me to join him to design the first microprocessor-based, multi-point, networked smoke alarm ever created for ADP. It was an exciting project! I was hand-coding assembly language for the new Z-80 microprocessor. Meanwhile, I bought my first investment property in Charlestown, MA. Shortly thereafter I bought another property. The real estate market was booming, and I was having a blast.

A visiting sales rep for the company who made the Z-80, Dana Burnham, was amazed that I was coding this entirely by hand in machine code. He promptly offered me a position to work for his company called Mostek.

Later, as the field applications engineer for Mostek, I made sales presentations for the sales force. I loved teaching in front of a crowd and then going back to the lab to solve difficult problems with other engineers. I noticed, though, that salespeople were making a fortune. In a pivotal life moment, I decided to become a salesman, and I approached the owner of the sales representative firm, Bill, for a personal meeting.

We sat down, and I told him, "Bill, I have been giving this a lot of thought, and I would like to get your opinion. I want to be in sales. I can sell like anyone else on the sales team, and I have the advantage of actually understanding the technology. Do you think you could add me to the sales team?"

I remember the look on Bill's face as he responded, "Mitch, great salespeople are born. They don't come along very often. Stick to being the best applications engineer, and leave the selling to us." Calmly I stood up, turned to Bill, and said, "Thank you for your time." Inside I was boiling.

I was so angry that he'd told me I wouldn't succeed that three words surfaced in my consciousness: "I'll show you…"

Later that month I enrolled in the Dale Carnegie Sales training course, which changed my life. I resigned from Mostek and became a semiconductor sales rep for a different rep firm while studying at night. I graduated with honors and quickly put my new skills to work.

I accepted this new sales position with a 50% cut in pay and, starting from scratch, spent fourteen months developing my accounts. Finally, after all those months of hard work, I received my first real commission check for $34,000! And those checks kept rolling in month after month. Remember, this was in 1982 and I was only twenty-eight years old. I opened bank accounts all over the city to deposit my checks since I knew that my money would be insured only up to $100,000 at each bank. I had a small pile of passbooks in my underwear drawer.

One day I received a report that shipments to my client were refused at the dock. That was the first sign of the downturn in the semiconductor industry. According to an experienced associate, the slowdown was normal, and business would pick up again in about five years. The writing was on the wall for me; in 1984, it was time for a new career.

At that time the IBM PC was starting to get very popular, and I decided to buy one. I started to develop software to keep track of the sample requests I received from engineers at companies building prototypes. It was fun, and it made the PC useful.

When I submitted the $5,000 I had invested to buy the PC as an expense, my accountant told me that the IRS would not allow it as a valid business deduction unless I had a record of every minute I used it for business – and an idea was born! I could develop software to track time!

Serendipitously, a young couple moved in next door a few months after I had bought a new house. I met Neil Ayer, Jr. who liked guitar and rock music as much as I did, and we became good friends.

One day, while having breakfast together, I shared my idea for a time-tracking app with him. He drew out a screen design on a napkin. After all, he was a professional programmer with five titles in the marketplace for the Apple II at the time. We had several more conversations, and six weeks later, he invited me to come over. He showed me a working prototype written on an Apple II clone in Pascal. I was elated!

Realizing the potential of our software, we started a company together: Timeslips Corp. After six months of development, I left my job to dedicate all my time to growing our business.

Then disaster struck. The IRS changed its ruling about contemporaneous record-keeping. Now we had a fully-developed product that was of no use anymore. Six months of our lives wasted! We were depressed, angry, and dismayed, but not for long. After brainstorming for a couple of hours, we came up with another use for our software. By adding just one field to the screen, a client name, the software would be able to track time that could be billed to clients.

In 1984 I visited Comdex, the Computer Dealer's Exhibition and one of the largest trade shows in the world. There I introduced our new software to the industry. Neil and I had each deposited $5,000 in a bank account as our entire investment. Nine years later, we were generating eight figures in revenue and had almost one hundred employees. The financial rewards, the friendships, and the countless lessons I learned made all the hard work worthwhile.

After we sold Timeslips Corp., I started investing in small companies while also providing them with business insight and helping them clarify their selling proposition and internal structures. I became the CEO of a local venture capital firm, ran a furniture-shopping business on the Internet until the market crashed, and eventually returned to my roots of helping companies succeed.

Life once again took an interesting turn of events when my friend Chet Holmes called and asked if I could help him recruit salespeople.

Using his method described in his incredible book *The Ultimate Sales Machine,* I tripled his sales force in six weeks and hired several strong candidates to run the division. When I told him I had completed the project, he asked me, "What am I supposed to do with this $18,000 check in your name? That is the percentage you've earned based on the sales of each person you've hired." I smiled. I continued to recruit salespeople, and I built a recruiting division. At one point we had five recruiters who worked for twenty different clients. Chet's powerful concept about Sales Superstars was so clever, it allowed me to build an entire system around it.

About nine months later, I became the president of Chet's company and joined in the negotiations with Tony Robbins to create Business Breakthroughs International, which we launched in 2008. We were growing fast. We had a powerful hiring system, and a well-designed and valuable product that people loved.

By 2010, our virtual call center was answering over three thousand phone calls a week. Life was good... until disaster struck. Chet was on vacation with his family in Mexico when he had to be rushed to the hospital and was diagnosed with stage four leukemia. After a fierce, courageous battle with the disease, he passed away sixteen months later in August 2012. I was devastated after losing my dear friend, mentor, and business partner of twenty-plus years. Earlier that year I was appointed CEO of the company and, despite my sadness, I was enthusiastic to make Business Breakthroughs International a world-class business "university."

Tony Robbins and I met at a hotel in San Francisco to discuss my plans to move forward past Chet's death to achieve our collective goals. Tony loved it, but unfortunately, Chet's family had other plans for the company, and I resigned.

Today, as I write these final words in this soon-to-be-published book, I am once again building a cutting-edge enterprise called www.ResultsBreakthrough.com which is focused on helping people find and keep accountability partners. Besides finding them, my patent-pending system guides them through their live interactions to ensure their success and progress. Currently I am working with several large training program publishers to include our system inside their programs so more people will get the benefits of what they teach.

My intention for writing *PowerTribes* is to provide you with the same tools and strategies that accelerated my growth and allowed me to create a better life for my family and me.

You see, I didn't come from a normal home. I didn't graduate top in my class or go to an Ivy League college. In fact, I should have been dead a long time ago. Yet my passion for life, my curiosity about the world, my appreciation for business strategies and technology, and my desire to rise above the modest means of my peers propelled me to blaze my own path in this world. It gives me joy to share my experiences, helping others to find a better way.

Thank you for reading *PowerTribes*. If this book has an impact on your life or business, I would love to hear from you. If you think my experiences can help you accelerate your own company, please feel free to contact me. I would be happy to speak on your stage, at your annual meeting, or to motivate your staff, your youth group, or your alumni.

Email me your success story, feedback, or questions. I would very much appreciate hearing from you. mitch@mitchrusso.com

To your success,

Mitch Russo